the EXCHANGE®

A Bold and Proven Approach
to Resolving Workplace Conflict

www.exchangetraining.com

the EXCHANGE ®

A Bold and Proven Approach
To Resolving Workplace Conflict

Steven Dinkin • Barbara Filner • Lisa Maxwell

CRC Press
Taylor & Francis Group

A PRODUCTIVITY PRESS BOOK

CRC Press
Taylor & Francis Group
6000 Broken Sound Parkway NW, Suite 300
Boca Raton, FL 33487-2742

Printed in the United States of America on acid-free paper
Version Date: 20110609

International Standard Book Number: 978-1-4398-5298-9 (Paperback)

Visit the Taylor & Francis Web site at
http://www.taylorandfrancis.com

and the CRC Press Web site at
http://www.crcpress.com

For Tara, Jim, and Mike, who continue to support

us in all of our endeavors. We are grateful.

Contents

The Authors

Steven P. Dinkin is president of National Conflict Resolution Center (NCRC). He received his law degree from George Washington University, where he taught a mediation clinic as an adjunct law professor. He has also taught mediation courses in the United States, Europe, and Latin America. For several years with the Center for Dispute Settlement in Washington, DC, Steve served as an employment and workplace mediator for the Equal Employment Opportunity Commission and other federal agencies. In 2003 he moved to San Diego to lead NCRC. His experience managing a talented and opinionated staff has contributed to the realism of this book.

Barbara Filner was the director of training for NCRC from 1984–2010. She has a master's degree in teaching from Indiana University and has worked as a teacher, a labor union official, and an analyst in local and state government. She has designed and conducted workshops on mediation and conflict resolution in the workplace in both the United States and Europe. She has lived in Pakistan, India, and Egypt, and thus brings a multicultural perspective to this book. She has also cowritten two books about culture and conflict, *Conflict Resolution Across Cultures* (Diversity Resources) and *Mediation Across Cultures* (Amherst Educational Publishing).

Lisa Maxwell has traveled all over the world as a senior trainer for NCRC, a position she held for almost 20 years. She is currently the Director of Training at NCRC. Lisa has a master's degree in education from San Diego State University and has developed curricula and taught courses at the high school and university levels. Lisa has worked with business, the military and nonprofit organizations on finding creative, effective ways to manage conflicts.

Acknowledgments

Our thanks to the following people who helped us in the writing of this book.

INSIDERS

Betty McManus, JD, helped us develop and edit the book from the time it was just an idea. Her time and her unflagging enthusiasm kept our spirits up throughout the book's creation. Her early editorial contributions also allowed us to have confidence in showing drafts to others.

Laura K. Walcher, one of San Diego's most accomplished PR professionals, has long been interested in NCRC and served on its board of directors. Her generosity, and her hours of careful editing, added spirit and clarity (and some carefully crafted sentences) to our work. Laura often asked us pertinent questions—especially, "What does this mean?"

Susanna Flaster and Nora Jaffe, members of NCRC's board of directors, and **Barbara Lee**, a friend and participant in an Exchange training, reviewed an early draft of this book and compared it to a semifinal manuscript. All three also provided their business savvy, which kept us from making some overly idealistic pronouncements.

Johanna Afshani, an attorney and a mediator representative on NCRC's board, read and commented on the book, made helpful suggestions about formatting and organizing chapters, and asked good questions about touchy issues such as confidentiality.

Trissan Maleskey is NCRC's paralegal, office manager, troubleshooter, and general go-to person. Her agility with all things digital helped us to format the document. We're also grateful for her patience with us as we wrote this book.

Robin Seigle, Director of NCRC's Business Division, was our best proofreader. She found many typos and misused words, and had a sharp eye for many other details.

The **NCRC staff** believed in us from the very beginning. At times they did extra office chores; at other times they stayed out of the way so the three of us could meet. They also took us to task when we became discouraged. We could not ask for a better team.

NCRC volunteer mediators, credentialing candidates, and panel specialists contributed cases, comments, and care for 25 years. Without them there would be no book.

OTHER PROFESSIONALS

Beverly Butler read and commented on an early version of this book. An experienced manager of several businesses and the co-owner of a contracting enterprise, she offered us an essential business-oriented perspective.

Scott Edelstein, editor extraordinaire, deserves much of the credit for shaping this book in ways that made it more readable and useful. His Web site *HelpingWriters.com* couldn't be more aptly named. We are lucky to have found him.

Tom Leet, Director of Human Resources at the University of California–San Diego, read and commented on the manuscript. Tom has been a supporter of NCRC for more than 20 years.

Mona Melanson, SPHR, is a freelance HR consultant who has lived in South America and Mexico. She offered many cultural insights, as well as knowledge of HIPAA and other relevant legal issues. She also read the manuscript and helped us tighten our message.

Charlie Pease is an expert witness and mediator who for many years served as a vice president at Merrill Lynch. His knowledge of how managers in large corporations think and what they need was extremely useful.

1

A Different Approach to Resolving Workplace Disputes

There is a time in the life of every problem when it is big enough to see, yet small enough to solve.

—Mike Leavitt, former United States Secretary of Health and Human Services

This book is about workplace conflicts and how to manage them. It is about the kinds of conflicts that drive a manager or supervisor crazy. They sap energy, affect productivity, and, in general, result in low morale, vast amounts of wasted time and high turnover. These conflicts, which occur in most workplaces, derive from personality styles, misunderstandings, and real disagreements. They may lead to an unhappy workforce, complaints, grievance hearings or even violence.

Do these examples look familiar?

- An employee receives a performance evaluation that she believes is unfair.
- A long-time programmer is passed over for a promotion for which she thinks she is qualified.
- The newest hire in a department is promoted to a supervisory position—but there are others who think they deserve the spot, including the longest-serving member of the team.
- An e-mail containing personal information about a coworker is inappropriately routed to the whole office, resulting in hurt feelings for the coworker.
- A scientist conducting experiments in a laboratory believes his partner is taking credit for his work.

These kinds of disputes, full of emotional complexities and interpersonal histories, are the headaches of the workplace. Yet these conflicts, when handled well, can result in creative resolutions that reenergize the workplace and bring new ideas to old problems. If you use the process described in the following pages, you will be able to solve most of these disputes quickly, while they are still small enough to solve.

WHO THIS BOOK IS FOR

This book is intended for the designated problem solvers, whether official or unofficial, in your organization. It is for all managers and supervisors who are held responsible for resolving disputes.

This book is for you if:

- You manage a workplace setting where you are responsible for dealing with other people's disputes.
- You'd like to be more than just a disciplinarian.
- You'd like some creative ideas and a better toolkit for handling workplace conflicts.
- You've had to put important tasks on hold because of all the fires that you need to put out. You'd also like to be more effective in dealing with those fires.

Like most managers, you probably did not set out to be a conflict resolver. You got your job because of your skills and successes—yet now you have to deal with others' conflicts and situations. You find it more than a little frustrating to be the fire chief. You are doing the best you can, but sometimes it feels like it's not enough.

This book will give you the strategies and skills to deal more effectively with such issues.

WHAT THIS BOOK OFFERS

This book introduces a process called The Exchange that will make your job easier.

We call this process The Exchange because it is all about exchanging understandings of facts, interests, feelings and solutions. It is a highly structured process specifically designed to encourage discussion of intense emotional issues in ways that are more productive than a gripe session. It includes constructive techniques to use in face-to-face meetings with disputing or disruptive employees. You can use this process to break down barriers—and to create changes that have a positive effect on your whole workforce.

If you want to know about the roots of The Exchange, skip to the end of the book and look at About The Exchange and Its Creators. If you don't really care where The Exchange came from as long as it works, welcome and read on.

THE EXCHANGE IN BRIEF

The Exchange is a four-stage process for addressing workplace conflicts. It involves a direct conversational exchange between conflicting parties— an exchange of facts, ideas, emotional impacts, and viewpoints. It begins with you and ends with all the parties coming together and developing effective solutions.

This is the process in brief:

- **Stage I: Hold Private Meetings**. You meet privately with each person involved to gather data and find out how each one views the situation. You also clarify your own stake in the resolution of the conflict.
- **Stage II: Develop an Issue List**. You organize what you have heard into a carefully framed list of topics. This will objectify the issues involved in the dispute and de-escalate some of the tension and emotions. You will use this list to help transform the dispute from an interpersonal conflict to a joint problem-solving discussion.
- **Stage III: Conduct the Joint Session**. You guide the people involved in a strategic discussion that takes them from the past to the future. This is the stage in which emotions are acknowledged and intentions are explained. In this stage you can help your employees reach a mutual understanding that brings new energy, new responsibility, and new vision to the situation.

- **Stage IV: Facilitate Problem Solving**. Here is where creative solutions emerge, resources are explored and commitments are made. This is the positive, concrete end to a problem that has taken up time and caused stress in your workplace. It is an opportunity to build solutions together.

FIGURE 1.1
The Exchange four-stage process.

These are goals of each stage:

Stage I: Hold Private Meetings

- Gather enough information to identify key issues and concerns.
- Prepare each employee for the joint meeting.
- Clarify your own stake in resolving the conflict.

Stage II: Develop an Issue List

- Develop a plan for the joint meeting.

Stage III: Conduct a Joint Meeting

- Help employees develop an understanding of how the situation has impacted each person—and the workplace as a whole.
- Clarify your own expectations.

Stage IV: Facilitate Problem Solving

- Identify and determine possibilities for resolving the issues.
- Create an action plan.

WHY THIS BOOK IS DIFFERENT

What makes this book unique and valuable? This:

As professionals who are regularly involved in solving workplace disputes, we know that:

- The responsibility for managing a conflict belongs to all of the parties who have a stake in resolving it, including the relevant manager.
- A structured approach is particularly helpful in working through conflicts.
- If there is to be a lasting resolution, the parties involved have to address the whole conflict, not just the surface issues.
- Emotions are important, not touchy-feely distractions, and they need to be taken into account.

We know how to deal with emotions—those messy, powerful, scary elements that tend to derail attempts to resolve conflicts in a tidy, rational way. We will share with you proven techniques that will help you deal with your employees' emotions—and your own—constructively and respectfully. And we will reveal a practical, sequential process in which there are no losers.

This structured method of dealing with disputes derives from the conflict resolution model we have used successfully as mediators for over 25 years. We have now adapted it specifically for the workplace. The heart of this process is a true exchange among the parties involved.

WORKPLACE CHALLENGES

Employees may spend as many of their waking hours in their offices as they do at home. And even at home, many employees find themselves tied to their work through their smartphones, computers and e-mail. Increasingly, people are expected to always be available—even during soccer games or dinner parties.

The result is that in the workplace itself, some coworkers become like siblings—peers who are competing for resources, including budget allocations for favorite projects, time with the boss and even promotion opportunities.

You and your fellow managers thus sometimes wind up serving in parental roles. You are blamed for whatever goes wrong because you somehow should have been able to avert all troubling situations.

The situation becomes even more complicated if you have been promoted to a position where you now evaluate former peers—a circumstance that is tailor-made for charges of unfairness or retaliation.

Underneath all these complexities is a single common thread: relationship.

Disagreements, disputes, and honest differences are normal in any workplace. When these normal occurrences are treated as opportunities for exploring new ideas about existing policies or projects, they can become a catalyst for increased energy and productivity. As Mike Leavitt points out in our opening quote, this most often occurs when a dispute is big enough to see but still small enough to solve.

When disagreements or disputes are ignored, denied, or dealt with in unproductive ways, however, they can escalate into serious conflicts that may result in hurt feelings, negative behaviors, and even lawsuits. And, of course, your organization's morale, productivity, and bottom line may suffer.

The ultimate goal of The Exchange is to fix a situation, not assign blame. Our experience has proven that when people truly understand each other's perspectives, they are more likely to find ways to work together. It has also taught us that the emotional aspects of any dispute must be addressed constructively. Otherwise, the unresolved emotions will lie in wait and come back to sabotage all the good work done on the issue. Those emotions will continue to flare up, sapping your (and your employees') time and energy.

The Exchange will help you preempt and de-escalate disputes early on, before they become volatile or intractable. In the chapters that follow, we will take you through every part of this process, one step at a time.

2

How The Exchange Works:
A Case Study

If you do what you have always done, you will get what you always got.

—Mark Twain

Mark Twain was right about a lot of things. Tom Sawyer and Huck Finn, those beloved characters from his books, were always getting into scrapes and finding new and innovative ways to resolve them. If you follow the stages and steps of The Exchange, you too will be able to resolve difficulties in new and innovative ways.

The following scenario, told from the viewpoint of a manager, demonstrates how The Exchange works. Each situation is of course unique, and each manager will develop their own style for using The Exchange—but you'll get a sense of how The Exchange can help resolve a serious conflict.

RESOLVING A DISPUTE AT HEALTH ALARMS

Background

You work in Employee Relations for Health Alarms, a company that specializes in monitor systems for the elderly, the disabled, and the seriously ill. Health Alarms began with off-the-shelf products such as talking pill boxes, video monitors, and bio-monitors for health checks. Strong and sustained sales have led to the development of a growing number of customized products.

An area of new and rapid growth for the company is a safety feature using high-tech sensors embedded in the carpet of residents' rooms at high-end retirement communities. Emergency services are automatically called when a sick, disabled or elderly person falls on the floor. This may save their life.

You are new to the company but have worked in high tech for many years. You see yourself as a people person, but you love gadgets and believe Health Alarms has a lot of potential.

However, there are ongoing tensions between the engineering and sales teams over what specialized features can and should be installed in a customized Health Alarms system. You have seen this problem before. Each team believes that it knows what the customer needs, and each member believes that without their department, the business would fail. In the last company you worked for, the sales team was the favored department. This led to many talented engineers quitting the company. You have also seen the opposite occur, in a company you worked for a decade ago.

At Health Alarms, you didn't know how bad things had gotten between the two departments until a recent status meeting, in which the director of sales openly accused the engineering department of being unresponsive and lazy. The head of engineering reacted by silently walking out of the meeting. Soon afterward, the rumor mill kicked in. Angry e-mails were sent to many managers and leaders, including the CEO. These accused the sales department of false advertising and lying to customers. The situation quickly escalated, becoming a huge drain on productivity and damaging the company's reputation.

Now the tension between the two departments has turned into outright war. In the cafeteria, employees in the two groups don't speak to each other. Various people have responded to the e-mails, siding with one group or the other. Other departments are gossiping about the conflict.

The CEO is furious about the situation. Because of your position and experience, he calls you and tells you to "fix it." He also wants to fire both Ginger (the head of sales) and Frank (the head of engineering), despite the fact that he recently hired Frank, who had been recruited by a headhunter.

You have to work hard to calm down the CEO and help him think more strategically about next steps. It is only when you mention the increase in sales because of Ginger's efforts, and the awards the engineering department received because of Frank's talents, that he realizes how much the company will lose if Ginger and Frank are fired. He still thinks that the head of engineering should be disciplined, however, because "he clearly initiated the e-mail circus." The conversation ends with the CEO saying, "I want this solved immediately. Take care of it."

Now you have a serious problem to work through.

Analyze the Situation

In thinking through the issues, you realize just how much is at stake.

You are not convinced that disciplining anyone will help, because the tensions go deep, and many people will be impacted. Punishment could even make matters much worse. You do need to remind people of policy issues—but, really, the issues are about respectful behavior, good communication, and achieving a common company goal.

This is also a big deal for you personally, because you want to prove yourself to the CEO. You also now know that, given his volatility and his demonstrated willingness to fire people, your own status within the company is uncertain.

You realize that settling this conflict is a job for The Exchange.

You learned The Exchange from your previous employer, where you then offered coaching and mentoring in the process to other managers. They would often come to you to discuss their Exchange strategies before they implemented them. (The engineers at your last company loved the structure The Exchange offers, while the sales folks loved the opportunities it gave them to communicate about issues.)

You call Frank, the head of engineering. At 6 feet 8 inches and 250 pounds, Frank commands respect. He has a no-nonsense way about him that you know slightly intimidates some people. But you also know that The Exchange can work.

Stage I: Hold Private Meetings

Welcome Frank: Thanks for coming in, Frank.

You acknowledge Frank's work and clarify the purpose of the meeting: You know, we're both relatively new to this company, but I do want you to know that I've been working in the high-tech field for many years. I knew of your innovations with sensor technology in the security arena before I came here. You bring so much to this company. I could talk about that all day, but I need to talk to you now about what happened last week. The tensions between your department and sales have really blown up, so I want us to work through these issues.

You explain how the process will work: This is the first step toward addressing and resolving those issues. I want to hear from you about what has been getting in the way of you and Ginger being able to work together effectively. I'll also be meeting with Ginger today. Tomorrow I want the three of us to sit down to discuss and resolve this matter together. I've reserved the conference room for 10:00 a.m.

You explain confidentiality, note taking and policies: I want you to know that I won't repeat to Ginger what you tell me unless you give me permission. I'm taking notes only for my records at this point. Of course, if any policy issues come up, I'll clarify those and take appropriate action.

You clarify your own interests: The situation has increasingly affected the entire production and sales teams, as well as people in other departments. We need to address it so we can get everyone focused back on the customized alarm systems, and on productivity. We also have to ensure that we have a comfortable work environment for all employees. I want to establish a good working relationship between the two departments, and between you and Ginger, and I want to improve morale for everyone on the team.

You ask an open-ended question to get Frank's perspective: So, tell me, what's going on?

Frank looks uncomfortable. He says: We're all for improving productivity, too. We just want to be able to focus on our work. In fact, that's precisely what we would do, if the people in sales would let us.

You repeat your request: That's great. But it really is important to me to hear your perspective on how the whole issue developed. Each department has unique contributions to make to the company, and these sometimes push against each other, so some tension is normal, and even helpful, at times. But this situation is harming the whole company. If we're going to succeed, we need to collab …

Frank interrupts: The sales team adds nothing to product design. They're a bunch of idiots who make false promises to everyone and his brother. They don't appreciate that quality takes time and that some things are just not technically feasible.

Just as suddenly as he began, Frank stops talking and folds his arms across his chest. You take a deep breath to remain calm.

Then you say: Tell me more about how things have gone for you with Ginger and her team.

Frank nods and says: Okay, well, I'm extremely frustrated by what they're doing. They make me look like the bad guy because of the ridiculous promises they make. They love the idea of the sensors in the carpet so much that they started telling potential customers that we could embed the sensors in rugs in the bathroom. That is just crazy.

Frank looks at you as if everyone in the world should know why that is crazy.

You acknowledge Frank's emotions and ask an open-ended question: Clearly, you're very frustrated with how the applications of our technology are communicated to potential clients. It's important that all of us are on the same page. Tell me some more about the bathroom application.

Franks sighs, visibly relaxes a bit and goes on: Well, the carpet sensors are a very complex combination of different sensory functions, you know—pressure, temperature, and motion. These enable the detection of someone lying motionless on the floor. If water comes into contact with the carpet, like if someone spills something, an intelligent safety system makes sure that the whole network isn't short-circuited, an occurrence that would trash the whole system. We can have that in the design for most areas, but we cannot have this system in an area that is virtually always wet. But sales is promising that we can design bathroom rugs with this system. The problem is that it WON'T WORK!

You demonstrate your understanding.

You say to Frank: So, it seems that you've designed a system that has this safety feature programmed in, but that system can't make up for large areas that are wet on an ongoing basis, such as a bathroom.

Frank nods and leans forward.

Frank says: Exactly. Now, we're working on some other sensors for near the toilet, shower and bathtub, but it's a different system. Sales makes us look bad because they promise it, and then we say, "Actually, no, we can't do that—and no, the new sensors aren't fully developed yet, and won't be for a couple of months." Quality control is really important. I won't have the Health Alarms name associated with a product that's on the market before its ready.

Frank looks you hard in the eye and continues: I know you people always say, "Did you talk to sales about it?" I have TRIED to talk to Ginger—I called her twice and left messages—but she is always so busy traveling the world on the company dime that she doesn't have time to talk to the people who design the stuff she's out selling.

You take a moment to absorb all the concerns that Frank has laid out and then demonstrate your understanding.

You say: I'm hearing that engineering recognizes the need for sensors in the bathroom and is currently working on some new innovations that meet the requirements of a wet environment. But these aren't ready yet, so we shouldn't be selling them. You also have some concerns about being able to communicate with sales. Have I basically got the picture?

Frank nods.

You continue: Just another quick question: Besides the calls that you made when Ginger was out of the office, can you tell me more about communication between engineering and sales in general since you joined Health Alarms? What has that been like?

Frank suddenly looks a bit uncomfortable and says: Well, I've seen her in the monthly management meetings.

He hesitates, then adds: But, you know, like I said, I really have been focused on my work.

You thank Frank for telling you his perspective; reiterate your interests; and ask Frank to consider possible solutions: I'm sure you've been kept quite busy with the new designs. Thanks for clarifying your point of view for me. My goal now is to find a solution to this situation that helps both of you, and both your departments, and everyone else at Health Alarms to work better together. Between now and tomorrow morning, why don't you think about ideas to resolve this that serve everyone's interests? I'm confident the three of us will be able to work this out. I'll see you both tomorrow morning at 10 in the conference room.

Frank mutters a curt "All right," says goodbye and leaves.

You take a five-minute walk outside to clear your head. Then it's time to meet with Ginger, a middle-aged woman who has the natural charm of a salesperson, but without an artificial air. She has a strong and powerful personality and is a natural talker.

You welcome Ginger and acknowledge her work: Thanks for coming in, Ginger. I got the e-mail from Neil about us landing the big Fortuna contract. I'm thrilled that we'll be doing the carpet sensors in a retirement community of that size and reputation. Great job. I'm really proud of our sales team—and, since you've been in charge, the team has done exceptionally well.

You clarify the purpose of the meeting: The reason I called you into my office is that I need to talk to you about what's been happening between sales and engineering. I talked to Frank just a little while ago. The tensions between your department and engineering have really blown up, so I want us to work through these issues. This meeting is the first step. I want to learn what's gotten in the way of your people and Frank's people working effectively together. Tomorrow I want all three of us to sit down and resolve the matter together; I've reserved the conference room for 10 tomorrow morning for that purpose.

You explain how the process will work, confidentiality, note taking and policies: I won't repeat anything you tell me to Frank unless you give me your clear permission. I'm taking notes, but those are only for my records at this point. Of course, if any policy issues come up, I'll talk about them and take appropriate action.

You clarify your interests: The situation has now affected a significant percentage of our employees. We need to get everyone focused back on their jobs and on productivity. We also need to have a good work environment, including a good working relationship between you and Frank, and between sales and engineering in general.

You ask an open-ended question to get Ginger's perspective: So, tell me, from your perspective, what's going on?

Ginger leans forward a bit and says, talking very fast: Well, first, let me thank you so much for the compliment about Fortuna. But customized sales are tough for us. Engineering will not communicate with us. They seem to look down on us. But, you know what? Without us, they could design all day, but there would be no one to buy their products.

    Honestly, I'm under tremendous pressure to outsell other companies with our products. And we are not the only game in town. At least we've been promised some good commission packages for our top performers this year. That helps. Plus, Neil has talked about maybe hiring some additional sales agents who are knowledgeable about customized sales.

You demonstrate your understanding, acknowledge Ginger's emotions, identify her interests, and ask a clarifying question: You obviously care a lot about your sales team. Yet I can hear that you feel there's a lot riding on your ability to make significant sales in customized markets. Tell me more about the concerns you have about that, especially as it relates to engineering.

Ginger launches immediately into her answer: We aren't engineers. We know about the products and how they work, more or less. But we get tons of special requests from these retirement places. We keep getting requests for bathroom sensors; you know, falls occur in the bathroom more than anywhere else. I got a special request when I was in Sioux Falls, so I called Megan and told her to go ask engineering. She asked Matt—you know, that ambitious young engineer we just hired in the spring. He assured her that engineering could embed sensors in anything. So, naturally, I told my customers that, yes, we could design something in their system that included bathroom rugs. Then, when I got back, Frank flew off the handle when I gave him the purchase order. When I started to ask him what was wrong, he yelled at me. We ended up losing the contract. Engineering just wants to sit on their laurels and not work on new innovations, even though they told us they would.

Clearly, there's poor communication between the two departments. Also, you suspect a bit of bravado on the part of Matt, who may have wanted to impress Megan. You say to Ginger: Here's what I'm hearing. You get a lot of special requests for system customizations, which you feel pressure to agree to, especially when someone from engineering has told you they're possible. You wonder about engineering's motivation to design new applications, and why they're not doing what they said they could do.

Ginger frowns and says: You know I'm a communicator. I've let myself get beaten up by picky customers many a time. But I will not be beaten up by the people I work with. Every time I try to talk to Frank, even about the weather, he's rude. He has no respect for me or what I bring to this company. He's a pompous, noncommunicative, negative jerk. He spends his whole day tinkering in the lab, and he has no idea what it's like to be on the road, day after day, dealing with demanding customers, while our competition tries to steal them away.

You decide to not challenge this verbal attack, but make a mental note not to allow such attacks in tomorrow's meeting.

You acknowledge Ginger's emotions and identify Ginger's interests: I can see how upsetting this has been for you. You expect to be treated respectfully by your colleagues, and you haven't felt that to be the case with Frank.

Ginger swallows and leans back a bit.

She says: I know I shouldn't have called him lazy in the status meeting, but I'd just flown in at two in the morning from a big conference in Miami. I was exhausted, and I was angry that I work so hard for this company, even giving up a lot of my personal time, and then he goes and treats me like he does. He doesn't know and doesn't care how much I do for Health Alarms. I have some good leads from the conference, but now I'm so worried he'll undercut me or not take me seriously. It's true that he's tried to set up a meeting with me since the big fiasco in Chicago, but I have to make up for that loss, and my travel schedule has been totally crazy.

Ginger is talking very fast and getting more upset. You know she needs to be acknowledged, so you say: Ginger, I want to reinforce that my goal today is to understand all of these issues from your point of view. So, you're saying that your lack of sleep affected your ability to manage a difficult situation at the meeting. Clearly, this company and our success mean a lot to you, and you care deeply about doing a good job. You also have concerns about your working relationship with Frank and the engineering department.

My goal in our meeting tomorrow morning will be to set up clear communication between the two of you so you can work collaboratively, without friction or stress, and so both of you have some new tools and understandings that you can draw on.

You give Ginger homework and ask her to consider possible solutions: Thanks for discussing your situation with me. Between now and tomorrow morning, I'd like you to think of some ways to resolve this that meet everyone's interests. One thing you and Frank have in common is that you both care a great deal about helping this company succeed. I'll see you tomorrow morning at 10 in the conference room.

Stage II: Develop an Issue List

In your office today, you heard two very competent professionals express how much their work and the company's success mean to them, and how deeply their work relationships affect them.

First you think about the issues. You make a list of the topics that must be addressed and resolved tomorrow:

- There needs to be a discussion about how the two departments will work together and share information in the future. Frank and Ginger—and their respective departments—need to find better ways to communicate with each other.
- Engineering needs to understand the pressure that sales is under with customized sales and customer relations.

- Sales needs to better understand sensor design, development, testing and quality control.

You realize that these topics will be easy to work through if each person can get beyond their resentments about the way the other treats them. That is why the employees will need to discuss the impact the situation has had on each of them.

You can see that a mutual lack of respect is driving the whole dispute. In some ways you are nervous about dealing with this. You are no psychologist, and you're not used to swimming in these waters. But as you think through the process to come, you remember that with The Exchange you don't have to fix other people's reactions, nor do you have to spend much time on them.

At the same time, if Ginger and Frank don't hear how this situation has affected each other, they will continue being angry. That's not an acceptable outcome. They each influence many employees and set examples— good or bad—for them.

You know that at the beginning of tomorrow's meeting, you will need to quickly establish the tone of the meeting, set the ground rules and announce the agenda. You also know that you need to begin with an icebreaker to get both people talking civilly to each other and to establish a positive tone. Both people are good at what they do and both care about the company, so you decide to begin by asking them what motivates them in their work for Health Alarms. You guess—and hope—that in their answers they will find some common ground.

Stages III and IV: Conduct the Joint Meeting

You welcome Ginger and Frank, clarify the purpose of the meeting, explain how the process will work, and establish ground rules. You say: Good morning. During the next 30 to 45 minutes, we're going to talk through the concerns that each of you has about working with the other. My goal here is to help the two of you be comfortable, get the respect that you each deserve, and get your people to work collaboratively. Specifically, we're going to talk about sharing information with each other; the challenges of customer relations; sensor development, applications, and processes; and how the two of you communicate with each other. We'll also talk about respect—and in this meeting we'll talk respectfully and honestly with each other to move past this. Agreed?

Frank and Ginger both nod their heads. Ginger shifts anxiously in her chair. Frank crosses his arms.

You start with the icebreaker and say: Let's start on a positive note—with what motivates each of us to work for Health Alarms. I'll start. I was working in Las Vegas when the computer and technology trade show was there last December. I went to it just because I'm a technophile. When I saw the Health Alarms booth, I knew it was a place I wanted to work. I loved the new innovations and I was fascinated by the sensors. I had read about their use in military settings, so when I learned about their applications in nursing homes and assisted living facilities, I got very excited. I went to the Health Alarms Website as soon as I got home. An Employee Relations job was open, and I applied and got it.

What about you, Ginger? What motivates you to work here—and to work as hard as you do?

Frank interrupts: Besides all the free vacations and traveling on the company dime?

Ginger looks at Frank and says firmly: You have no idea the pressures I have when I take these trips. They're no vacation.

She takes a breath, turns to you, and says: You know, I don't mind traveling so much because I really believe in our products. I think our off-the-shelf products, especially the talking pill box, are great. But when we started making the sensors, that's when I knew I wanted to build my career here. My 96-year-old grandmother insists on living on her own, and she has them in her apartment. So, for me, this is personally a very important product. I like to sell things that I believe in; that's how it works for me.

You look at Frank and ask: What about you, Frank? You're fairly new here, like me. What brought you here?

Frank uncrosses his arms and lines up his papers on the table.

Looking down, he says: It's not about the money for me, either. I believe in making a difference. After we designed the sensors for security applications at Defense Carpeting, it was just a matter of fine tuning that technology for other uses. For me, the idea of utilizing this application for seniors and handicapped people was very attractive. But quality control is equally important to me. That's what really drives me: the opportunity to develop high-quality products that people can not only use, but trust and believe in.

You want to tie together what both people have said, so you acknowledge commonalities and say: It's interesting how all three of us are driven by these products rather than just by money or position. Ginger, I had no idea that one of your own family members used a Smart Alarm product. And Frank, I'm impressed at how you think about giving our customers something they can believe in. So, Frank, I wonder—have you ever considered that the sales team, or at least Ginger, sells the products you design because she believes in them?

Frank looks directly at Ginger and says, unemotionally but emphatically: I had honestly never considered that possibility.

Ginger looks at Frank and says: Well, I do believe in them. Very much.

You seize the moment by beginning a discussion about impact and ask Ginger to say how the situation has been for her: One of my goals here today is to facilitate communication between the two of you, so you can share important information with each other. This has been a real issue. One thing that's clearly getting in the way is that you both feel the other is not treating you with respect. How has this been for you, Ginger?

> *Ginger takes a deep breath. For a moment, she seems nervous about expressing herself to Frank.*

She looks at Frank and the words pour out: You think you're so much more important than I am just because I'm not an engineer, but I'm important to this company, too, whether you like it or not. You've been trying to—

> *You need to regain control of the situation because Ginger has just attacked Frank instead of describing her situation.*

You interrupt her, firmly but politely: Excuse me, Ginger. I know this is difficult, but I'd like you to focus on how the situation has affected you. Please remember to talk respectfully. I want to make sure that you're being heard in the way you want to be heard. Frank, when Ginger is done, I'll ask you to repeat the key points she's made, to make sure that they all got communicated. Go ahead, Ginger.

Ginger nods and begins again: I'm sorry. I have to say that it's very stressful for me. I'm not accustomed to someone disrespecting me the way you have. Frank. I worked hard to get to the position that I have, and I believe in these products. Truthfully, I was shocked by how you acted when you started working here a few months ago.

Ginger pauses here, so you turn to Frank and ask: What points did you hear Ginger make, Frank?

Frank, who has been taking notes, looks down at the legal pad in his lap and says, in a perfunctory way: She said that she is stressed; that she thinks I don't treat her with respect; that she worked hard to become the head salesperson; and that she doesn't like the way I treat her.

> *You note that Frank and Ginger have taken the first step to building greater understanding.*

You ask Ginger: Ginger, is that what you wanted Frank to hear?

Ginger replies, sounding a bit disappointed: Yes, I guess so—though I'm not sure he gives a damn about any of it.

Frank blurts out: I was asked to repeat what you said, and that's what I did, Ginger. No fanfare about it. That's how I do things.

You decide to not give Ginger a chance to react to that. Instead, you move forward by asking Frank how the situation has impacted him: How about you, Frank? How has the situation been for you?

Frank looks at you, not at Ginger, and says: The issue for me is that I don't like it when customers are promised things that I can't do. That makes me look bad. My reputation and our products' reputations are important to me.

You turn to Ginger and ask: Ginger, what are Frank's main points?

Ginger looks at you as she says: It's about Frank's reputation. He doesn't want us salespeople to make unrealistic promises, because they make him look bad. Which I completely respect and get. I have no interest in making false promises, either. I have integrity, too, you know.

You turn to Frank and ask: Frank, did Ginger capture what you wanted her to hear?

Frank sighs and begins to relax. He says: Yes, actually, she did.

Ginger looks at him and smiles slightly.

You transition to expectations by asking Frank: What were your expectations for your job when you started here, Frank?

Frank snorts and chuckles briefly. He says: Well, I expected I would have free rein to design, you know, my own private science lab, with lots of R&D money that I could use to make a difference. That was a rather foolish expectation, I guess. I mean, it's never that simple. And I understand that we need to make a decent profit. But I've never complained about it, and I've always done my best work for the company.

Frank's comments appear to soften Ginger a bit. Allow an interruption when the topic is productive.

She looks at him and says: You're right, it isn't that simple. And I've never said you weren't doing your best work. But we need you to not only do your best, but to continue innovating. I have nothing to sell if you aren't creating new and better products. From the time you first got here, I expected you to keep us in the loop about what we could and couldn't offer in our customized sales. We aren't engineers; we get requests and do the best we can for our customers. That's our job.

Ginger takes a breath and continues: Remember that purchase order I gave you from Sioux Falls for the sensors in the bathroom rugs? Did you know that we asked one of your engineers—it was Matt, I'm almost positive—if that was possible, and he told us that you guys could embed sensors in anything. Well, that's what I told the customer. And you know what I thought at the time? I thought, "Man, those guys in engineering are total wizards." If you'd walked into my office then, I would have thanked you and kissed you on the cheek. And then you accused me of over-promising!

> *Frank chuckles again and looks at Ginger. It's not a threatening look, but a look of respect.*

He says: I didn't know Matt said that. He's such a headstrong fellow; he reminds me of myself at that age. I'll have to talk to him. So I guess that part was our screw-up. But I do try to keep you informed. It's just that you're always traveling, and when you are here, you want me to come to sales meetings. I'd rather go to the dentist than to endless meetings. I like things that have some logic to them.

Ginger laughs and says: Well, I'm not sure I really want you at a meeting! But is there some way our departments can have an ongoing liaison—you know, like an engineer who likes meetings? Does that kind of person even exist? Also, it would be so helpful to have someone to call when we're with customers in the field, someone who can be an advocate for us.

> *Some good communication is finally starting to happen—and some momentum is building. You identify Ginger's interests and move to problem solving.*

You say to Ginger: So, it would be important for you to have someone in engineering who communicates regularly with your sales team?

Frank is making more notes. Without looking up, he says, in a surprisingly friendly tone: Ginger, remember Ajit, the engineer who retired a couple of months ago? Well, I got an e-mail from him last week. Retirement is a bit boring for him, he says. Great engineer, nice guy. What do you think?

Ginger nods and says: Yes, great guy. Very charming, even though he's an engineer. Are you thinking he's the liaison type?

Frank looks at Ginger. He seems pleased that she is problem solving with him. He says: Well, maybe part-time, if I get the budget increase

I've been promised. He can answer technical questions, do basic explanations to the custom sales staff, and be the go-to person. Also, he can keep the younger guys' feet on the ground. He can even go to your meetings instead of me.

You say: I know that upper management has been talking about hiring two or three custom salespeople. I can push them to add Ajit half-time as well. He's a natural fit.

Ginger nods and says: I like it. Ajit not only knows how to communicate, but he speaks three languages. With our growing international sales, that could be a real asset.

Clearly, a breakthrough has occurred. Instead of seeing each other as opponents, Ginger and Frank have begun to communicate. They are now colleagues trying to find solutions to the challenges they face. The rest of the conversation will be easy.

You let the discussion continue, allowing Ginger to go into a long explanation of customer relations, and letting Frank hold forth on sensor technology and new applications. Then you suggest that they consider some job shadowing for interested team members to give everyone a better appreciation for the other side of the process. Both agree to this. Without your prompting, they also work out how their departments will communicate with each other in the future. Frank also promises Ginger a projected timeline for the innovations that engineering is working on. They even decide what they will share with their departments about this meeting.

Next Steps

You end the meeting by saying: Thank you both. We've made a lot of progress in this meeting. I want to thank each of you for your hard work and your willingness to talk through and resolve these issues. I'll check in with each of you in a couple of weeks to see how everything is going.

Within two months, Health Alarms makes immense progress. Ajit rejoins the engineering team three days a week. Every month he publishes a customer wish list for both departments that serves as a feedback loop between sales and engineering. The departments, once at war with each other, now have bi-monthly meetings attended by Ajit, Ginger, and other interested engineers and salespeople, at which they discuss any issues that have emerged. Engineering now publishes regular product road maps for sales to use. These describe the features of new products and provide timelines for products that are in development.

Last week, Frank and Ginger both thanked you for bringing them together using The Exchange. You are very satisfied with the outcome. So is your CEO.

SOME FINAL THOUGHTS

The Exchange is a dynamic process that adapts to different people, situations and conflicts. If different people had been in conflict, the meeting would surely have gone differently, and you might have said and done different things. But you would still have followed the same essential process.

Similarly, had someone else run the meeting with Frank and Ginger, they might have said and done different things than you did. But if they used The Exchange, then they would have followed the same basic process you did.

In the rest of the book, we will walk you through every part of The Exchange. By the end, you will have a new set of tools—and be well equipped to create more positive results.

3

Getting Ready

Conflict in its most basic sense is inevitable, the source of all growth and an absolute necessity if one is to be alive.... Adults don't seem to know how to enter it with integrity and respect and some degree of confidence and hope.

—Jean Baker Miller, Toward a New Psychology of Women

Even smart, successful people sometimes fail to understand how important it is to treat fellow employees respectfully. As we saw at Health Alarms, people don't usually think about how their words and actions might affect others. They just do what comes naturally, especially if they are feeling ignored or undervalued. The unintended consequences can be very serious.

The Exchange reduces the chances of creating these consequences and helps participants create productive working relationships that encourage confidence and hope. This process also gives you, the manager, an opportunity to model integrity and respect, which can then spread to the rest of your workforce.

It is well known how chronic conflict drains morale in the workplace. Jean Baker Miller is absolutely correct that most adults don't know how to participate in a conflict with respect and dignity. Bringing this respect and dignity to a conflict is part of what The Exchange will teach you. It's also part of why it works—and what you will demonstrate to others when you use it. In the process, you will also teach them to bring the same respect and dignity to future conflicts.

Managers make decisions, set standards, monitor behavior, evaluate performance and do countless other things. When you use The Exchange, you also take on the role of problem solver. This role requires a new mindset. We don't suggest that you forget any of the knowledge or skills that make you a good manager. However, The Exchange will require you to use your current knowledge and skills in a new way.

As the facilitator of The Exchange, you will likely need to be more indirect than you are used to being. For the most part, you will be asking, not telling, and most of your questions will be open-ended. In the process, however, you will find out important information about your employees that most managers don't usually get to know. This includes information about their motives and interests.

By "interests," we mean the underlying needs and desires that motivate people to say or do particular things. They are what a person wants, needs or hopes for from someone else. Interests are often unspoken, but they are always present, and they strongly influence what people say and do.

When you and your employees better understand the effects of one person's words and actions on another, the foundation is laid for creating lasting solutions to problems. As a result, once an Exchange is complete, conflicts are resolved and everybody wins, including you. This is quite different from typical workplace battles, in which one side is perceived to win and the other side appears to lose.

In this chapter and the ones that follow, we'll describe each of The Exchange's four stages in detail. We'll also show you a variety of useful techniques and how to implement them, and we'll give you some examples of how each of these has been used successfully by other managers.

Preparing to conduct The Exchange involves three steps:

1. *Assess* the effect of the conflict on your workplace and its employees.
2. *Clarify* your own interests, roles, and responsibilities.
3. *Schedule* private meetings with the key people involved in the conflict.

Let's look at these steps one at a time.

STEP 1: ASSESS THE SITUATION

The Exchange works well with most ongoing conflicts. However, if the people involved seem likely to work things out satisfactorily without your involvement, let them. Don't be a micromanager.

Similarly, if the conflict is so deep and seemingly intractable that it requires an outside consultant or a lawyer—or if litigation seems likely—then it probably can't be resolved through The Exchange.

However, if the conflict is somewhere in between these two extremes, as most workplace disputes are, it's probably a good candidate for The Exchange.

Conflicts in the workplace do not magically appear. They tend to develop slowly and then deepen. Often as these conflicts escalate, they take on lives of their own, because one or more of the people involved can't back down without losing face. Opposing camps may develop. Sometimes employees stop speaking to each other. (This dynamic can continue even after the original disputants have left the organization or patched up their differences.) This might have happened at Health Alarms if Frank and Ginger had been fired instead of guided to a resolution using The Exchange.

As you assess the situation, then, here are some questions to ask yourself:

- Who are the key players?
  What are their roles in the organization? Does one have a higher status than the other? Does one report to the other? Has one been employed longer? What do you know about their personalities?
- What are the behaviors that concern you?
  What do the disputing employees accuse each other of doing? To the best of your knowledge, what did each one actually say and do? What have you seen or heard each of them do or say? How are other employees reacting to the dispute, and to each of the key people in it? Are you aware of any gossip related to the conflict?
- Has a company standard or policy been violated?
  If so, by whom, in what way, and how often? Do the violations need to be reported to anyone else—e.g., HR or your organization's legal department?
- What are your other options for constructively managing the situation?
  Does your organization have a formal grievance process? If so, is it appropriate for this dispute, or will it be overkill? Has it already been used? If so, why didn't it work?
- What will likely happen if you do nothing?
  Is this something that will likely blow over if you ignore it? Will other conflicts flare up if you don't do something? Will some upcoming

> *event or situation force a solution—or create a potentially bigger conflict?*

- Is this the appropriate time for you to step in?

  Is there a good reason to wait a bit longer and see what happens? Or does the conflict require prompt attention? If you don't do something now, will one of your superiors likely intervene? What would that mean for the conflict? For the disputants? For you? For your organization?

- What is the worst thing that could happen if you *do* intervene now using The Exchange?

  How likely is it that one or more of the disputants will quit? That you will need to fire someone—or multiple people? Will other employees see your intervention as harmful? Why?

- What are the best possible outcomes of your involvement?

  What would it be like to be able to do your job without thinking about this dispute? What if the disputants were able to support and help each other? What if you could show your employees that it's worth dealing seriously and respectfully with workplace conflicts?

In our experience, there are few conflicts where it would simply be *wrong* to use The Exchange. Even if a conflict is a simple misunderstanding that might eventually get cleared up without any intervention, a brief Exchange can often shorten the process of resolution and save everyone time and trouble. On the other hand, a significant dispute that is left unaddressed can sometimes escalate into widespread antipathy, investigations and even lawsuits.

If your assessment leads you to decide that it is important to address the conflict now, and The Exchange seems like the right process to use, go on to the next step.

STEP 2: CLARIFY YOUR INTERESTS, ROLES, AND RESPONSIBILITIES

Before you meet with anyone, meet with yourself. As the facilitator of the upcoming Exchange, you need a strategy that fits each of the personalities involved, including yours. Also, as a stakeholder, you are also going to be affected by what happens.

Throughout The Exchange, you will represent your organization. You will also be the facilitator of the process.

In using The Exchange, you will share the responsibility for making things better with those who created the conflict. This makes it less likely that another dispute will occur and escalate, because you will have modeled conflict resolution skills for the participants, and encouraged and empowered them to share the responsibility for resolving the conflict.

Holding the meetings of an Exchange is an art, not a science. Don't create a decision tree or a script—even a loose one—and then try to get people to follow it. This not only won't work, but it could worsen the problem. Instead, simply keep in mind that you and the other participants share in the responsibility for creating an acceptable resolution. We also encourage you to suspend judgment about what should or could happen at any particular moment.

At the same time, however, as a participant you need to think about what results *you* want to see. You will then need to work toward those ends. Of course, you want to see the dispute resolved. But you may also have some more personal goals. For example, you may want to demonstrate your conflict resolution skills to your boss—or you may want to position yourself for the raise you plan to request.

Lastly, if you approach the issues and the people involved with integrity and respect, your chances for success are astronomically higher than if you use the old hierarchical "Do as I say" approach.

None of this preparation takes much time—perhaps half an hour. Think of this time—and The Exchange itself—as important investments in your organization's success. In the long run, The Exchange typically saves managers untold hours of time that might otherwise be taken up with investigations, disciplinary sessions, or firing people and hiring replacements. The Exchange thus serves as a form of quality control and risk reduction.

STEP 3: SCHEDULE PRIVATE MEETINGS WITH THE KEY PEOPLE INVOLVED IN THE CONFLICT

You will have brief consultations of about 20 minutes each with each key person in the dispute. (In the vast majority of cases, disputes will have two sides, and each side will have one key person. Sometimes, though, there may be three or even more sides to the dispute, and/or more than one key person from each side whom you'll need to meet with.) You will also hold one joint session lasting 30–60 minutes.

The one-to-one sessions should be held as close together as possible, preferably on the same day. The joint session should be held a day later, or as soon afterward as possible. This will give each person enough time to think through possible solutions and consider any questions you raised in the one-to-one meetings—but not so much time that they can obsess at length over the conflict or make it significantly worse.

When should you meet? If the most convenient time for someone is after hours, check to see if the employee will need to receive additional (or overtime) pay. If this is so, you will need to either spend the extra money or insist on meeting during business hours. We should add that it is usually best to meet during the work day, so that other employees can see that the simmering conflict is being addressed. (There may also be contract or collective bargaining issues to take into account when scheduling meetings. If so, of course respect and follow the relevant rules.)

Where should you meet? Somewhere private, quiet, convenient, nonthreatening, and comfortable. Privacy is especially important. A conference room with a door that can be shut is ideal. If an employee is worried about coworkers seeing or overhearing the conversation, they are much less likely to be forthright. It is difficult to build trust in a conversation if you are worried that what you say might come back to haunt you.

Your office may also be a good place to meet—but only if, when you issue the invitation, it doesn't sound like you're summoning the person to the principal's office.

It's important that the meeting place have comfortable seating arrangements. These help create a mood of collective problem solving, rather than of being taken to the woodshed for punishment.

How you invite people to attend one-to-one meetings sets the tone for how the situation will be resolved. So do it in a friendly, problem-solving, low-key way. Be cordial, open, and nonthreatening. For example, "I'd like to talk with you for a few minutes about the situation with _____. Does 10 a.m. tomorrow work for you?"

A private face-to-face invitation is much better than an e-mail, which can be forwarded to others and then take on a life of its own. A private face-to-face invitation is also better than a phone call, because with a phone call you can't control who may be in the employee's office at the time.

USING THE EXCHANGE: GETTING READY

As we look more closely at The Exchange, we'll follow four different workplace conflicts. We'll watch as managers handle them, one step at a time, using The Exchange, and you'll see how The Exchange can save you time, money and stress.

CONFLICT #1: THE SPACE RACE

Two programmers on the same work team, Trisha and Vivian, have adjacent cubicles at Quality Plus, a large technology consulting firm. Both are in their mid-thirties; both are quite confident about their abilities. Trisha works quietly, without talking much to others. Vivian is much more social. A frequent project leader, Vivian is known for her creative approaches. She spends a lot of time networking to get ideas and test out potential strategies.

Trisha and Vivian are constantly feuding about anything and everything: the way they spend their time at work; how efficient (or inefficient) each is; what constitutes "professional communication"; and even what should and shouldn't go on the cubicle walls. As Trisha and Vivian become more frustrated with each other, other team members are getting drawn into the conflict. Pedro, the department manager, is concerned about the worsening morale, and decides to use The Exchange to address the problem.

In analyzing the situation, Pedro notes that the quality of both Vivian's and Trisha's work has noticeably slipped in the past month or so. Both are making more errors in reports, and they recently missed an important deadline. Both also go through the day with sullen faces. Pedro needs both programmers, who have different but complementary skills. Their current project is for Auto Universe, which has asked Quality Plus to redesign their computer analysis programs for designing aftermarket auto parts. The president at Auto Universe has made it quite clear to Pedro that he expects to receive Quality Plus's best service and highest-quality work. He tells Pedro that he expects him to settle this situation between the two programmers quickly and quietly.

Near the end of the day, Pedro visits Trisha and Vivian in their cubicles and schedules private meetings with each for the next morning, as well as a joint session for the following afternoon.

CONFLICT #2: MANNERS OR MEANNESS?

Images and Icons is an electronic equipment manufacturing business with clients all over the world. Patty, an administrative assistant in the sales department at I&I's national headquarters, complains to HR about how rudely she is often treated by Tom, one of the company's sales representatives. HR contacts Norita, a seasoned administrator who manages both employees. Norita asks for the opportunity to handle the situation using The Exchange; HR agrees. Norita hopes to not only resolve the situation, but to improve her own chances for promotion in the process.

Norita considers Patty to be one of the best administrative assistants the firm has ever had. Patty is thoroughly professional. At age 26, she is considerably younger than some of the staff, but she has earned a reputation for working hard and being willing to do whatever the department needs. Norita knows that Tom can be prickly, but also knows that he consistently brings in a lot of money. Tom is in his mid-50s, and tends to talk in quick bursts, as if he is issuing orders to a platoon of soldiers.

Norita stops by Patty's office and schedules a private meeting with her for the next afternoon. Tom is out in the field all day, so she calls him on his cell phone. The two set up a meeting just before lunch the next day. Because Tom is out selling much of the time, Norita decides not to schedule the joint session yet.

CONFLICT #3: DON'T SHIFT ON ME

In the maternity ward of Springwood Medical Center, there has been a history of tension between Norma and Danelle, the supervising nurses in charge of two consecutive shifts. While both are excellent nurses, they have very different administrative styles. Norma, who is in her 50s, is quite traditional and formal in how she treats patients and staff, insisting on letter-of-the-law adherence to hospital protocols. Norma's uniform is always neatly pressed, and she is adamant that her nurses meet the hospital's dress code whatever the weather or time of day. Danelle, who is 39, is much more informal. She's a spirit-of-the-law person who tends to overlook what she considers minor infractions by staff, especially when the ward is busy.

Some of the younger nurses find Danelle's style more comfortable, and two recently asked to be transferred to her shift. In response, Norma accused Danelle of "stealing" her best nurses.

A new computerized patient tracking system has been recently installed, replacing the old-fashioned handwritten charts that Norma is comfortable with. Danelle is eager to work with the electronic system, but Norma has accepted it only grudgingly. She has also raised questions about how well it can accommodate the special situations that can quickly arise when a patient exhibits fetal distress.

The simmering conflict between the two supervisors erupts during a meeting of all the maternity department's managers regarding the new patient care procedures required by the electronic system. Norma and Danelle begin to argue about filling their shifts in light of the changes. The meeting is disrupted as their voices grow louder and each accuses the other of undermining her authority. Maryanne, the department head running the meeting, quickly takes control of the discussion, and realizes that the conflict needs to be dealt with quickly.

After the meeting, Maryanne considers the dispute. She recognizes how important it is that everyone uses the new patient tracking system properly and effectively. This is not an administrative issue, but one of patient safety. She knows that if the dispute is not resolved, patient care may be compromised, and the hospital's reputation— and her own—may be damaged.

Maryanne speaks separately to Danelle and Norma, scheduling individual meetings with both supervisors. She also finds a time between shifts when both women will be available for a joint meeting.

CONFLICT #4: WHO GETS THE JOB?

Brad is the operations manager at a small private energy company, Sun Systems. Brad has been besieged by complaints from department employees in the aftermath of a recent promotion decision. The review committee unanimously chose Mike to become the director of the engineering department, even though Mike has the least seniority of any of the final candidates. Mike, who has worked at Sun only three years, is a confident 40-year-old who walks with an easy gait. His office is filled with piles of blueprints, and everyone knows that he has plans for both himself and the company. The other internal candidate, Simon, has been with the organization for 15 years and received consistently good performance reviews throughout that time. He tends to speak hesitantly, as though unsure of himself, but no one has criticized the quality of his work. He has occasionally been late in meeting deadlines, however. Simon now complains to anyone who will listen that the selection process was unfair. Mike is angry, too. He feels that he has been thrown into a hornet's nest, simply because he has worked hard and well for the company. He has started to complain about the complaints. Employees are beginning to form camps in favor of Mike and Simon.

Brad, their manager, realizes that his own career in the company will suffer if the dispute is not settled quickly. On Friday morning he stops by Mike's and Simon's offices and schedules private meetings for Monday and a joint session for Wednesday morning.

4

Holding Private Meetings

Any time we can't solve it, we have to manage it, until we can start to solve it again.

—Tony Blair, former British prime minister

Stage I of The Exchange, the private meetings with each employee, is where you get to find out what the conflict is really about from the perspectives of the key people involved.

These meetings are an effective way to do what Tony Blair suggests—begin to manage a conflict before trying to resolve it. The resolution won't (and can't) occur until the group meeting, when the key people are sitting together in one room.

In each private meeting, it's important that you devote your own undivided attention to the other person. Don't allow interruptive phone calls or visits, and don't try to multitask.

Each private meeting needs to be long enough for you to gather some real and useful information—and, ideally, to make the employee feel a bit more comfortable about resolving the dispute. Fifteen to twenty minutes is usually about right. If the meeting is too short, the unexpressed message is that the situation really isn't that important. If the meeting is too long, it can turn into what feels like a deposition, an investigation or a therapy session.

Explain at the beginning of each meeting that this is an opportunity for the employee to speak freely and confidentially. In some cases, this may be the first time someone in authority has taken time to hear what the employee has to say without criticizing them.

It may also be important for the employee to be allowed to talk without interruption, at least for a limited time. You may be surprised to discover that when you provide an attentive ear and a safe place—somewhere

where the conversation cannot be heard by others—employees will open up to you.

In these meetings, you are looking to gather information—not only the facts as each employee perceives them, but the motivations and emotions that lie behind their actions. You also hope to understand the interests of each party—what they really want or need. Later, in the joint meeting, you will use this information to help your employees create a personalized solution to the dispute.

This one-to-one meeting also allows each employee to privately express what they believe is most important. Each person may need to say some pretty harsh things about the other before they can take a more objective view of the situation. Let them do this. Don't defend the other person or try to explain their viewpoint. Simply let the employee speak. It is better that they say these things to you now than to the other person later. Indeed, these initial private meetings partly serve to siphon off anger and frustration—and, thus, to prevent people from verbally abusing each other (or losing face by appearing weak) in the joint meeting.

Every culture, and virtually every employee, has concerns about saving face. When people believe they are at risk of seeming weak (or, even worse, stupid) in front of a perceived adversary, their natural tendency is to puff themselves up, sound indignant and defend their point of view. In such situations, they can easily change their goal from resolving a difficult situation to defeating a perceived enemy—or at least putting that person in their place.

If you were simply to call the people together to talk about the situation without this private meeting, at least one of them is likely to feel attacked or threatened. They may then shift into a defensive mindset that will make any collaborative resolution difficult to achieve. That's part of why these initial private meetings are so important.

As a conflict develops and escalates in a workplace, each person begins to construct their own evidence to support their position. The two disputants rarely share this evidence with each other, however. Soon, there are at least two distinct versions of the situation. Both versions may have some truth to them, though adherents of one version might characterize the other version as a lie. In your private meetings, you will likely get a good sense of each version.

These private meetings are also personally important for *you*. In the later joint session, you don't want to get lost or bamboozled—or to lose face yourself—because you didn't know enough about the situation or each employee's perspective on it. By listening to each person privately, you will learn how to frame the joint discussion topics in ways that will advance agreement rather than erect new barriers.

You have four tasks to accomplish in each private meeting:

1. Establish rapport and confidentiality.
2. Hear the employee's perspective.
3. Identify the employee's interests.
4. Discuss the next steps.

Let's look at each of these tasks in detail.

TASK 1. ESTABLISH RAPPORT AND CONFIDENTIALITY

These private meetings are not formal investigation sessions. Keep them informal and conversational. It helps if you are relaxed, but attentive and concerned. Don't rush. Most people will be nervous for the first few minutes. Let them be nervous.

Start by explaining the purpose of the meeting: to collect information and understand the situation better. Emphasize the confidentiality of any personal information the employee may share with you. For example:

> *Thanks for coming. I want to talk to you about _____. This situation needs to be dealt with, and I'd like to hear how you see it and what ideas you may have to resolve it.*
>
> *I'm also meeting with _____ to have a conversation like this with them. Then the three of us will meet together for 30–60 minutes to create a workable solution.*
>
> *This will be a private conversation. I won't repeat the information you share with me to anyone without your permission unless there's been a violation of organizational policy, in which case I'm required to report it.*

There will be other aspects of confidentiality for you to consider (and, as appropriate, to mention to employees). For example, if an employee gives you any personal medical information, you may only share it with the appropriate HR person, not with the other employee, under HIPAA privacy regulations. And if you work in a government agency, you may be required to report issues of fraud, waste or abuse.

If you plan to take notes in the meeting—which we recommend—say so. Explain that these are strictly for your own use and won't be shared with anyone (again, unless there's been a violation of organizational policy). For example:

> *I'm jotting down a few things so I don't forget what's really important when we get together for the joint meeting tomorrow. I'll be doing the same thing when I meet with _____.*

Taking a few notes conveys the message that the meeting—and what the employee says—are important to you. But keep your note-taking minimal—i.e., write down only the most important things. Don't write complete sentences; use bullet points. Taking too many notes can convey the message that you are creating a record. Besides, if you are too focused on making notes, you won't pay full attention to the employee.

TASK 2. HEAR THE EMPLOYEE'S PERSPECTIVE

After you have explained the reason for the meeting and how The Exchange will work, ask the employee for their perspective on the dispute. Then simply listen attentively without saying much. This will usually encourage the employee to keep talking—and will send the message that you are genuinely concerned about them and the dispute. At this early stage, this is also the best way to get good information.

Unless you simply can't follow what the employee is saying, don't interrogate or ask questions. If you do, the conversation may turn into an interrogation or a mini-investigation. You run the risk that the employee will shut down, only answer direct questions, and not reveal anything more.

Effective listening involves more than not talking. Messages are conveyed by body language and tone as well as by words. Since you want to convey to the employee that you are genuinely concerned about the situation, think about how you are sitting—lean forward and make eye contact. Keep physical barriers such as desks to a minimum. A desk implying power for the one behind it sends a very different message from chairs around a conference table where the playing field is level.

When the employee has finished, or when you begin to hear the same information again, it's time for you to speak and respond respectfully. Keep these three points in mind:

First **demonstrate** that you understand by briefly and straightforwardly recapping the employee's main points. For instance:

> *I want to make sure I've heard you correctly. You haven't been able to get your work done because of what feels like chaos around you. Things aren't where you left them. Even your computer gets used by other people when you aren't there. You're convinced that Charlotte wants your job and may be trying to sabotage your efforts. Is that the essence of the situation?*

Avoid saying things like, "I understand where you're coming from" or "I get what you're saying." People won't believe that you understand just because you say you do. But they *will* believe it when you demonstrate your understanding by accurately recapping their primary points.

Don't worry if you don't get these points exactly right. In fact, it's often helpful if the employee corrects you, because this gives them a chance to add some further details to the story, or to talk a little more and vent more of their anger or bitterness. (Interestingly, in these one-to-one meetings, most employees will simply *explain* what they might feel forced to *defend* in the presence of their disputant.) It's less important that you hit a bull's eye with your comments than if your tone conveys real interest in and curiosity about what your employee has to say. If you haven't heard something fully or correctly, you can be sure the employee will try again to make sure you do.

Next, **acknowledge** what you think has been the effect of the situation on the employee, and let the employee respond briefly. For example:

> *It sounds as if this has been extremely frustrating and confusing for you. Or, What you're saying is that you feel disrespected, unappreciated and ignored. Have I got that right?*

Then pause briefly to listen.

If you need more information about the situation at this point—and you probably will—don't ask for lots of specific details yet. Instead, ask open-ended questions—questions that require more than a one- or two-word answer. For example:

- *Could you say a little more about the situation?*
- *What happened next?*
- *Is there anything else about this issue that you want me to know?*

Then confirm again what you heard from the employee, both to make sure you've heard it correctly and to let them know you've heard it correctly. The best way to do this is to once again quickly recap the key points. Don't repeat the whole story, just its headlines.

Then check that your understanding matches theirs. Ask, *Did I get everything?* or *Do I have a clear picture of the situation?* This check for accuracy verifies that what they said was what you heard, that it mattered to you and that you respect the employee.

If you need to, at this point you can go deeper by asking a few more specific questions about the conflict.

These three techniques: listening effectively, responding respectfully and going deeper with open questions are the key techniques of Stage One.

TASK 3. IDENTIFY THE EMPLOYEE'S INTERESTS

Next, make sure you understand what the employee wants, expects or hopes for—and what they feel they haven't gotten. This information is often the key to resolving the conflict.

In any workplace, these are people's typical interests:

Having their input valued. Employees want to be able to provide input on issues and decisions that affect them and their jobs. In particular, when a conflict involves supervisory styles, employees often feel that their input isn't sought or valued.

Autonomy. Employees want to be able to make decisions, however small, that improve the quality of their work. This is why micro-managers often face resistance from employees even when they are "only trying to help." We don't like to be told what to do in too much detail—especially when we think that what we're told to do adds no value to our work.

Fairness. People want to feel that they are being treated equitably, and that they are being evaluated by the same standards as everyone else. This is the underlying interest in many cases that involve promotions, hiring practices, job assignments or the division of workload.

Acceptance. Most people want to be accepted by their peers and their bosses—and they want to be valued for who they are and what they do. Many disputes that are supposedly about discrimination are really about how people believe they have been treated. Are they respected and valued as parts of the workforce, or are they seen as outsiders or expendable widgets?

Getting a chance to succeed. Employees want to know that they have the abilities and opportunities to succeed at their assignments. Have they received adequate training, equipment and support? Have they been given clear and reasonable roles, assignments and instructions? Do they feel confident that they can do what needs to be done? If not, they will feel set up for failure. This is often reflected in missed deadlines, high absenteeism or negative attitudes.

Being treated respectfully. Of all our nonphysical needs, the need for respect is perhaps the most important. An employee who feels disrespected is never going to do their best work—or, in some cases, any work at all.

Sometimes an employee may not clearly realize what their concerns or interests are. You can help them discover these by asking questions based on what they tell you. For example:

- *So, for you a key concern is the fairness of the process?*
- *It sounds as if you really want to be able to have some input into these decisions. Would you say this is true?*
- *Are you saying that you'd like to be treated more respectfully by _____? Would this help the situation?*
- *If you were acknowledged for your contribution to this project, would that make it easier for you to work with those folks?*

By sounding tentative, and/or by asking a question, you implicitly give the other person permission to correct you—and to explore the thought further.

Remember, though, don't ask too many questions in a private meeting. You don't want it to feel like an inquisition. There will be plenty of time for more questions later, in the joint session.

TASK 4. DISCUSS THE NEXT STEPS

Thank the employees for their thoughts, and remind them of the upcoming joint meeting—or, if that meeting hasn't yet been scheduled, propose a time and place for it. Ask them to spend some time between now and the joint session thinking about how the other employee might view the situation. Also ask them to try to come up with some solutions that might work for both people. For example:

> *Thanks for talking with me about the situation. It's helped me get a better sense of what's going on. We'll have a chance for both of you to clear up some things tomorrow. Before then, I'd like you to think about how _____ sees the situation and what the two of you might do together to resolve it. Let's plan to meet tomorrow morning at 9 in the conference room. I'll confirm this with you after I've met with _____ and checked on her availability.*

TIPS FOR PRIVATE MEETINGS

Don't offer advice about the situation—or talk about what someone should have or could have done, or should or could do in the future.

Once an employee starts speaking, **don't interrupt**. Respect that they will say what needs to be said in the way they need to say it. Save any clarifying questions for later. But you *can* ask encouraging short questions like "And then … ?" or show that you are listening by saying, "Uh, huh."

Don't give any opinion—positive or negative—about the topic or the person not in the room. If you appear to be defending anyone, the employee may see you as biased and unfair.

Stay nonjudgmental. Remember, you are only hearing part of the whole story. Don't come to any conclusions yet. The employee will sense if you don't approve of their position, and their instinctive reaction will be to shut down and become defensive.

Monitor your tone. Keep it friendly, informal, and relaxed. Also monitor how the employee is reacting to you. Do they seem relaxed and confident, or uncomfortable and resistant? Are they talking easily, or are you working hard to get them to speak?

USING THE EXCHANGE: HOLDING PRIVATE MEETINGS

Here's what happened next in each of the four conflicts introduced at the end of Chapter 3:

Conflict #1: The Space Race (two programmers on a project team work in adjacent cubicles—and get on each other's nerves)

In private meetings, Pedro learns that Trisha is missing some important documents, and believes that Vivian may have taken them. To emphasize her territory, Trisha has put a line of masking tape between her and Vivian's cubicles. He also learns that Trisha, who serves as the bookkeeper for the project, can't concentrate on the numbers while Vivian plays music with a strong beat in her cubicle.

For her part, Vivian, who is the project lead, insists that the music helps to stimulate her creativity. As for the many personal phone messages that Vivian makes—and Trisha resents so much—they are mostly to Vivian's fragile, elderly mother, whom she is temporarily caring for.

Pedro discovers that each woman feels that the other is deliberately interfering with her ability to do good work. He also learns that both programmers feel honored to be working on this important project. They both also fear being taken off the team and moved to something less challenging or important.

Conflict #2: Manners or Meanness? (one employee accuses the other of treating her rudely)

In a private meeting, Norita discovers that Tom, the sales rep, has no idea why Patty, the administrative assistant, is so upset at him—though it is clear to him that something is bothering her. She has stopped greeting him when he checks in, and she routinely turns back to her computer when he tries to initiate a conversation. From his perspective, Tom treats Patty as he always has, although he admits that recently he has been under enormous pressure to close some big sales and has been spending a lot of extra hours at work. Norita also learns that Tom's wife has threatened to divorce him for working so many hours.

As for Patty, she tells Norita that she is used to being acknowledged and praised for her ability to run the office so efficiently. Tom, however, doesn't seem to notice or care. In fact, when Tom wants her to do something for him, she feels that he demands rather than requests it, as if she is his personal servant.

Conflict #3: Don't Shift on Me (a simmering conflict between two nursing supervisors over a new computerized patient tracking system and employee loyalty)

In a private meeting, Maryanne confirms the rumor that Norma believes Danelle is "stealing" her best nurses by promising them an easier work shift and a better patient ratio. Norma is also afraid that the new tracking system will make her look bad because Danelle has much more experience in working with computers.

Maryanne also discovers that Danelle was surprised to have received applications for shift reassignments from two day-shift nurses. When Danelle spoke with both nurses, they had told her their current supervisor had become a micromanager. They liked the day shift, but they didn't like the atmosphere Norma had created.

Conflict #4: Who Gets the Job? (the promotion of a relative newcomer over a talented company veteran)

During his private meeting with Mike, Brad learns that Mike was specifically recruited from another energy company three years earlier by Sun Systems' former CEO, who is now retired. The former CEO promised Mike the promotion as soon as the position became available. However, Mike does not feel he should be the one to say this to Simon. Mike also speaks of his many years at another company that have prepared him for the job—and that give him more total years of relevant experience than Simon. Mike is angry that no one seems willing to let him prove himself.

When Brad meets with Simon, he learns that Simon was encouraged to protest Mike's promotion by a friend in another department, who feels that seniority should always be the key to promotion. In fact, Simon is a bit relieved that he didn't get the promotion, because the new job includes supervising other people, which Simon doesn't like. "But people talk," he says. It soon becomes clear to Brad that

Simon worries about losing face in front of his colleagues. "They think I've been screwed, and they worry that they'll be screwed, too, when they're up for their own promotions." It's clear that he wants a reasonable way to talk about why he didn't get the promotion, something that will satisfy the others in the department.

5

Developing an Issue List

The opportunity for cooperation is there, even in our most vexatious
disputes, if we'll only bother to look for it.

—William Raspberry

You have now heard two points of view, and you have a sense of where
these coincide and where they diverge. You have also had a chance to identify the concerns that each person needs to have addressed.

Now you have reached Stage II of The Exchange, where you will create a
working agenda for your joint session. This agenda, called an issue list, is
also a strategy for encouraging positive dialogue.

An issue list frames the specific topics in the conflict, and the emotional
impacts these have on each individual involved. These are described in
nonescalating language, so that everyone can constructively discuss them.
In The Exchange, the issue list is the first chance to develop an "opportunity for cooperation" to which William Raspberry refers.

At the heart of your issue list will be a neutrally stated list of topics to
address in the joint session. By combining each person's issues and concerns into this one list, you help all participants in the room focus together
on solving the problem, rather than on the typical demand-and-conces-
sion bargaining from separate positions.

The National Conflict Resolution Center developed this concept in the
early 1980s. It has proved to be a highly valuable tool for solving disputes
efficiently and effectively.

In an issue list, you combine people's separate *internal* perspectives into
a jointly owned problem to be examined and resolved together. By doing
this you reduce individuals' personal attachment to their positions. This
makes it easier for them to engage in constructive problem solving.

Thus you *externalize* the problem. You change the situation from one in which each person holds a particular viewpoint that needs to be defended into one in which an externalized problem affects both the people, and the organization they work for. Complaints are morphed into concerns that need to be addressed. All of you can then analyze, discuss, and resolve this problem together.

To be able to externalize issues into a list, you will need to use language that's different from what you used in your private sessions. We call this *nonescalating language*, because it generally keeps conflicts from escalating. It's language used to break down barriers, not create or strengthen them.

We call this brief, informal document an issue list because it's an easy name to remember—but an issue list actually has three parts: the initial **icebreaker**; the **impact** that the conflict has on the people stuck in it; and the actual **issues** involved.

In your joint session, you'll deal with these items in the order in which we listed them above. But in *creating* an issue list, you'll work in the opposite direction. You'll begin with the issues, proceed to the impact, and then, last of all, create the icebreaker, based on the other items on the list.

ISSUES

These are the specific concerns that employees first talked about in their private sessions with you. These form the substance of the dispute.

When you first heard these issues, they probably sounded like complaints or accusations. Now, however, you're going to frame them in neutral terms.

The key is to include both people's viewpoints within the same issue. Here are some examples, taken from the ongoing conflicts we've been following:

Complaint	Issue
Tape between cubicles (The Space Race)	Personal boundaries at work
Rude treatment (Manners or Meanness?)	How people treat each other
Stealing employees (Don't Shift on Me)	Keeping nurses satisfied with their jobs
An unfair selection process (Who Gets the Job?)	Getting the best person for the job

When you reframe a complaint as an issue, you give employees a sense that they have both been heard, but neither has been judged. You will be pleased to learn that few disputes have more than four essential issues, and many have only one or two.

List the issues in the order in which you wish to address them in your joint session. There's no one-size-fits-all strategy for doing this. Often, however, issues form layers. Resolving (or even just discussing) one may set the stage or build the necessary rapport for dealing with another.

Don't make your description of any issue too detailed. That can sometimes feel quite intimidating to employees. Keep each issue simple. The point is to assure the disputants that their major concerns will be addressed.

IMPACT

The impact of any dispute is the emotional responses that have blocked all attempts to resolve the conflict. If you can respectfully manage your employees' emotions, you will be in a good position to move forward.

In most conflicts, there is a reason (or more than one reason) why things haven't been resolved. Typically, this has very little to do with content, and almost everything to do with feelings—especially anger, frustration, resentment and/or disappointment. These often result from one person's expectations of how the other person should have or could have responded to something. Often, each person also makes assumptions about the motivations behind the other person's actions.

Sometimes managers want to quickly reach a solution by asking disputants to put their feelings aside. This is a huge mistake. Acknowledging emotions is an essential part of The Exchange. Trying to ignore them only makes them seem *more* important to the person who feels them.

You can't fix people's emotions—and, really, you don't need to try. In any case, The Exchange is not therapy. You don't have to dig deep into people's pasts or analyze the underlying causes of how they feel. Instead, you simply accept the reality of their emotions and understand that they bring energy to the dispute. In The Exchange, you will use this energy to help create a satisfactory outcome.

In The Exchange, you don't get pulled into people's emotions or let anyone get stuck in venting, blame or criticism. However, it's essential that each person hears the personal and emotional impact that the conflict has had on the other. (Most employees never stop to consider that the conflict has actually taken a toll on *both* people.)

Acknowledging emotions doesn't require you to make them points of direct discussion. In fact, you shouldn't. Just as you transformed complaints into issues, here you will morph emotions into impacts, using nonescalating language suitable for the workplace. For example:

Emotion	Impact
Both people feel they have been treated unfairly	Both people believe the policy of workplace equity has been violated
Both people feel disappointed by the other	Each person had expectations that the other person did not live up to
Both people are upset because they think the other is sabotaging them	Each person is no longer willing to rely on the other
Bob feels jealous of Judy because she's the CEO's niece; Judy is jealous of Bob because he's the department head's best friend	Both people believe that in their organization connections matter more than performance

Non-escalating language sends a message that the issue can be talked about without having to be debated. It uses words that lead to understanding, cooperation, shared meaning, and agreement, rather than to more arguments.

ICEBREAKER

Most people come to a joint session ready to complain, debate or argue. They have marshaled their most compelling arguments and are ready for battle. If you go straight to the topic of controversy, most people will quickly get stuck in defending their positions and attacking their opponents.' That's why you need to do something different. In The Exchange, you begin with an icebreaker.

This is not just a light introductory activity. In The Exchange, it is a way to nonconfrontationally initiate a conversation about difficult issues.

Typically, an icebreaker comes out of what you have heard in private meetings, but is not central to the conflict. Instead, it is an inquiry into people's professional experience. For example:

- *I'd like to start our conversation by going back to what originally inspired each of us to go into this field. For me, it was _____. What about you, Frieda? What was it for you?* (Listen while Frieda responds.) *What about for you, Li Pao?*
- *You've both said that this project is an important stepping stone in your career. Let's talk for a minute about how each of you views your role in the project. How about you, Abdul? (Listen while Abdul responds.) And how do you see your role in the project, Gary?*
- *Let's begin by taking just a minute to talk about this company and what we each feel it offers to the industry.*
- *What does each of you like about working here?*

An ideal icebreaker asks for each person's own take on something that's both work-related and positive. Many of the best icebreakers involve the organization and/or the employee's role in it, so that it may yield some new information relevant to the discussion.

Here's an icebreaker that often works when both employees have worked on the same project together:

> *This is an important project for our organization. I was glad to see that you were both assigned to it, because it's the kind of challenge I've always wished for. Remind me how you both got involved.*

An icebreaker should not be something that can be disputed or corrected. It should also be easy for people to talk about from their own experience.

A good icebreaker works in multiple ways:

- It gives each speaker a chance to strut their stuff, and to remind the others in the room of their value, abilities, and/or interests.
- It encourages each speaker to say (and think) something positive about their job and/or their organization.
- It gives each person an opportunity to hear something positive about their opponent—and to see that their adversary might have a positive trait or two.
- It brings out and highlights some commonalities that the disputants may have ignored, forgotten, or not realized.
- It may give you new information or insights that you can use to craft a workable solution. It may also help you better understand how and why the conflict emerged, and/or what is at stake for each employee.

- It gives the parties a small window of time to step away from the problem and just listen to each other. It may be the first time in quite a while that either has heard anything positive from the other person.

Your issue list is the plan that will guide everyone in the room and create opportunities for cooperation.

AN EFFECTIVE ISSUE LIST ...

- Reflects the relevant issues; acknowledges the emotional impact of those issues; and includes a relevant, positive icebreaker.
- Is brief rather than detailed. A typical issue list includes 1–3 issues, 1–3 impacts, and one icebreaker.
- Uses neutral, professional, nonescalating language.
- Combines both sides into shared issues that externalize the conflict, framing it as a problem to be solved together rather than as two contrary positions to be adjudicated.
- Lists the issues in the order in which you will discuss them.
- Serves as an agenda or road map for the upcoming joint session.

USING THE EXCHANGE: CREATING AN ISSUE LIST

Here are the issue lists that managers created to help solve our four ongoing disputes:

Conflict #1: The Space Race (two programmers on a project team work in adjacent cubicles—and get on each other's nerves):

Icebreaker: Talk about a project you've worked on here that you found especially satisfying.

Impact: What has been the effect of this situation on you? On your performance?

Issues: Personal boundaries at work; being part of an effective, productive team; meeting the goals of the Auto Universe project

Conflict #2: Manners or Meanness? (one employee accuses the other of treating her rudely):

Icebreaker: What initially attracted you to your job here?

Impact: How is this situation affecting your work? Your relationships with coworkers? What were your expectations about how you would be treated by your coworkers? About how you should treat them?

Issues: How do reporting relationships affect interpersonal etiquette here? How can people in this company better demonstrate their respect for one another?

Conflict #3: Don't Shift on Me (a simmering conflict between two nursing supervisors over a new computerized patient tracking system and employee loyalty):

Icebreaker: How did you first get into nursing?

Impact: What has been the effect of this on you? On your performance? On your relationship with employees who report to you? How would you have wanted the other person to handle the situation?

Issues: Supervisory styles; staffing for each shift; getting on board
with the new computerized tracking system

Conflict #4: Who Gets the Job? (the promotion of a relative newcomer over a talented company veteran):

Icebreaker: Simon, you've been here for 15 years. What's kept you
here? What about your job is still challenging for you?
Mike, how did you get involved in this field?
Impact: What did you expect the Selection Committee to decide—
and why did you expect that decision?
Issues: What does the department most need in a leader? What is
the role of seniority in promotion? What criteria do the
Selection Committee use in making decisions, and how
transparent should the committee be about them?

6

Stage III: Conducting the Joint Meeting

We can't solve problems by using the same kind of thinking we used when we created them.

—Albert Einstein

Now it's time for the three-way conversation—the joint session. This conversation is going to be different from other conversations you've had with your employees. You'll be using different thinking and different tools than you have generally used in the past. Einstein would surely approve.

You'll also use different communication tools than the ones you use when you are acting strictly as, say, an administrator or department head or team leader. In this joint meeting you will not only represent your organization's interests; you will also play the role of facilitator. Your job is to change the direction of the conflict, from escalating tensions to forging workable solutions.

In this conversation, you will use the same informal, cordial, nonconfrontational tone you set in the private meetings. This conversation will *not* be a pity party or therapy session. The three of you will analyze the problem, explore options, and create a mutually satisfactory course of action.

Start the meeting by welcoming both people. Acknowledge that they are taking time away from other projects to attend the meeting, and assure them that it will be well worth their time. Remind them that resolving the dispute is important to you and to the organization, as well as to them.

Next, very briefly name or outline the situation in a single phrase or sentence. Mention that you have learned some important details from each of them in your private meetings, and that these will be helpful as you work to resolve the issues.

Then bring out your issue list. Read the items in the "issue" section of the list. Mention the tangible, concrete, specific topics that the employees raised in the one-to-one meetings.

Here's one example of how these opening minutes might flow:

> *Glad to see you both. As you know, we're here to talk about and resolve the situation between engineering and sales on the McLeod project. I know how busy you both are, and I also know that this situation has hurt productivity and morale in both your departments. If we work together, we can all be out of here in less than an hour, with a solution that satisfies everyone. To do this, we're going to follow a process that's different from what you may be used to. Here are the issues we need to cover if we're to be successful:*

Read and very briefly describe the issues on your issue list. If there are more than four, read and briefly describe only the most important three or four.

Next, begin the three-way discussion by using your icebreaker. Be sure to use yourself as an example first, so you can model how to respond. It's likely that both employees are looking to you to figure out what to do. So be relaxed, friendly, straightforward, and very brief. For example:

> *I'd like to step back just a bit. When we started this project, part of what excited me as the team leader was the idea that it was a completely new direction for this company—and that the entire team, including me, had been hand-picked because of our particular skills. I'd like each of us to talk briefly about why we were chosen to work on this project.*
>
> *In my case, it was because of the project for the Wisconsin casino that I headed up—and for completing the project early and under budget. I assumed I'd be expected to save as much time and money as possible on this project, too.*
>
> *Amy, tell us about some of the skills you bring to this project, and about the original expectations you had for your role in it. (Amy does as she is asked.)*
>
> *Thank you. And Oscar, what skills do you bring to the project, and how did you originally think you would be part of it? (Oscar responds.)*

Be ready to intervene with a "thank you" the very moment each speaker completes their response—and before they have a chance to add "but."

"But" can completely negate anything positive that preceded it—and it can cause the conversation to veer off. Don't let this happen.

Now move to the impact of the situation. Don't forget to start with your own perspective; you are both a role model and a participant in this process. Especially in the beginning of the meeting, when the individuals in conflict are still a bit nervous about being together, they will be looking to you to figure out what to do. A good transition is a one-sentence summary of what you learned from the icebreaker. For example:

> *It looks like each of us got involved here because we had something unique to contribute that would help the organization, while also helping to advance our careers. And yet, now things aren't working the way they should. Let's talk about why...*

As you now know, your employees' feelings have to be addressed before they can craft a workable resolution. Yet in The Exchange you are not a therapist or counselor. Nor are you a parental figure who comforts or salves wounded spirits. Instead, at this point your job is to simply guide your employees to recognize and respect emotions as a part of the dispute.

This means getting both employees to tell each other what the effect of the conflict has been on them. Without agreeing with, endorsing or denying the other person, each employee simply needs to notice that the situation has affected the other person in a negative way. This *must* happen before the three of you can explore possible solutions.

The best way to encourage this is to serve once again as a model. Tell the employees what effect the conflict has had on the department, division or other unit. Only then should you ask them to talk about their own situations. Here are some examples:

- *I'm concerned about the lack of progress we've been making on the project, because you two, who are the keys to its success, have not been working together. I'd like for each of you to talk briefly about the effect this situation has had on you. Eunice, would you start?*
- *This situation has had a negative effect on the whole department. Productivity and morale have both suffered. I've had to put out several fires that grew directly out of this dispute. That's taken time away from my other duties as a manager, and that bothers me. What's it been like for each of you as this conflict has grown? Marta, why don't you talk first?*

- *Our CEO has been on my case about this situation—and he should be, because it's starting to hurt morale. I'm eager to resolve the situation so everyone can breathe easier. I'd like to find out how this dispute has affected each of you. Antonio, would you talk about its effect on you?*

In The Exchange, avoid words such as "emotions" or "feelings," which sound too much like therapy. Instead, use nonemotional words such as "concerns, reactions, and effects." Some examples:

- *When the problem first appeared, what was your reaction?*
- *What are your own concerns about the situation?*
- *What effect has this had on you and your work?*

Pick one employee and ask them to speak first. If the other employee tries to interrupt, tell them calmly but firmly to wait until the other employee finishes. Remind them that they will have their own chance to speak, uninterrupted, very shortly.

When the first employee is finished, immediately thank them; then, quickly turn to the other employee and ask for their reaction. Say something like:

> *My guess is that you were affected differently. Talk about your own responses and reactions to the situation.*

Your job now is to make sure that each employee genuinely understands how the other experienced the situation. To do this, summarize how the situation affected each employee—and check to make sure that your summary is accurate. (If you like, you can briefly include your own personal reaction in your summary—but focus mostly on employees' reactions and the impact on the department. If you say too much about your personal reaction, you may distract people from listening to each other.) For example:

> *It's clear that this situation has gotten seriously in the way for both of you, reducing the trust that each of you have for each other, and also reducing your enthusiasm for your jobs. Tom, you were embarrassed by being singled out in front of the whole staff, and Patty, you were really stunned by his response, which you experienced as disrespectful. Did I get all this right?*

You may want to take this a step further, by asking each employee to summarize the other out loud, so that each knows that the other truly does understand. Indeed, there are few things more helpful for breaking down barriers than hearing your adversary express an accurate understanding of your situation. Such an expression sometimes leads directly to a sincere apology and a quick resolution of the conflict.

When people explain the impact the situation has had on them, they also usually acknowledge, at least by implication, what has been blocking a settlement of the dispute. It also helps people show—and receive—respect by recognizing that the conflict has taken an emotional toll on everyone in it.

Some employees won't want to discuss this emotional toll in the joint meeting. But if *you* describe the emotional costs for both parties and get them to agree that you have accurately described the situation, that often works just as well—and, in some cases, it works even better, because you save people the embarrassment of having to say it themselves. This simple act can sometimes make it possible for both parties to move on to a resolution.

Now it's time to talk about the issues. These will become your bridge from conflict to resolution.

Start by being sure that all three of you mean the same thing when you think and talk about each issue, just as you did when you talked about the effects of the situation on both employees. Put the issues on the table clearly, directly, and succinctly. It's fine to read them aloud from your issue list. Then pick the first issue and say:

> *Let's deal with this first. Our goal right now isn't to resolve anything. We'll get to that in a few minutes. Right now we're just making sure that all of us see each issue in the same way.*

Ask each person, one at a time, to briefly describe their thoughts about the first issue, then to talk about its relevant concrete details. As before, let each person talk without interruption from you or the other employee.

If both employees define and discuss an issue in similar terms, they may be ready to begin a substantive discussion about how to resolve it. But normally this won't happen yet. Instead, you will read the next issue aloud, and have each employee, one at a time, briefly talk about that issue and their thoughts about it. You'll do this, one issue at a time, until you've gone through all of them. The goal here is to make sure both employees share a clear understanding of all the issues before moving on to problem solving.

You will develop your own style. The key essentials in this stage are to develop a dialogue and understanding before meaningful problem solving can occur, and to make clear that employee participation in the discussion and solution building are essential.

If the two employees express starkly different views of an issue, however, you might ask each person to comment on what they expected from the other when the issue first arose, and how this expectation differed from what actually happened. Here are some things to consider:

- **What message did each mean to give to the other?** Were specific requests made that were not responded to? Did someone hint at what they wanted instead of asking directly? (Not everyone is good at deciphering hints and implications.)
- **Was there a disagreement or misunderstanding over what steps needed to be taken?** Sometimes different people make different assumptions about where a project is headed or what needs to be done. Each may assume that the other understands and agrees— yet, because there wasn't a full, clear conversation about it, different visions of the situation may have developed. No one meant to deceive the other, yet someone may feel sabotaged and the other may feel falsely accused.
- **How did one person interpret the other's reaction?** How accurate was this interpretation? How much of that interpretation was based on assumptions or inferences?
- **Does someone feel mistreated?** If so, your role is to help both employees be as clear and specific as possible about the situation. Ask for concrete details. For example: *Can you talk about an incident when he acted that way? What did he do and say?* Once an employee has presented a specific example, the other employee can talk about what they intended by their actions.
- **Are you monitoring your own language?** In describing the situation, avoid using words that reinforce negative conclusions. For example, instead of saying *"So you felt mistreated,"* say *"You wanted to be treated fairly."* By using words that are neutral (or at least less explosive), you avoid turning the discussion into a spiral of accusation and denial.

If a discussion reveals a misunderstanding and/or an inaccurate assumption, point this out. Then ask how the employee might have responded differently—and what the result of that response might have been.

In talking about each issue, we also encourage you to use the tools you used in your private meetings:

- **Acknowledging**: recognizing the effect of the situation on each employee.
- **Asking open-ended questions**, such as *Could you say more about that?* and *What happened then?*
- **Summarizing** before transitioning to the next issue (and before the discussion begins to go in a circle).

Issue by issue, you will guide both employees through this process, with one person at a time defining and developing the issue, and then both employees discussing it until they agree on what the issue is and why it is important.

Occasionally, it may be necessary to take apart a big or complex issue and talk about each piece of it, one piece at a time. One way to begin doing this is by outlining the separate parts yourself:

> *Obviously several things went wrong with this project. Let's start with how it started losing focus back in February. Then we'll look at the specific assignments, the scheduling, the input from the executive team, and the feedback session afterward.*

One potentially beneficial variation on this theme is to build consensus around one or more of the component parts. For example:

> *From what both of you have said, the whole presentation went awry from start to finish. Let's look at what was involved, piece by piece. Obviously, you both agreed on the concept. But then there had to be a design phase. Sam, what was involved in the planning?*

Sam describes the planning stage. You nod and continue:

> *Okay, thank you, Sam. What are your thoughts about what Sam has just stated, Sarah?*

After Sarah has spoken, you can ask another question that zooms in on specific pieces of the issue:

> *Sarah, did you have a hand in this planning, or did you get involved later? Was that the next phase after the initial planning, or did something else happen in between?*

Sarah comments. Next you give Sam a chance to add his perspective.

> *Okay, and then what had to happen after that before the project was ready to be unveiled at the convention?*

Remember that you and your employees are not yet working to resolve anything. You're just making sure that everyone agrees on what the issues (and, perhaps, the pieces of the issues) are, and that they both understand each issue in the same way. Once this understanding has been reached, however, it's time to move on to problem solving.

Remember, don't spend time second-guessing what *could or should* have happened—it's too late for that. If your employees begin the blame game of "*If only you had …,*" jump in and move the conversation forward. For example,

> *We can't change what happened, and it doesn't make sense to spend much more time on the past. But we* can *do something about what happens now—so let's use this time wisely and move into what needs to happen.*

USING THE EXCHANGE: CONDUCTING THE JOINT MEETING

Some highlights from the beginnings of the joint meetings for all four conflicts:

Conflict #1: The Space Race (two programmers on a project team work in adjacent cubicles—and get on each other's nerves)

The conversation begins after Pedro asks each person to describe their favorite project for the company (**icebreaker**), and to discuss the effect of the current situation on them (**impact**). He then says:

Pedro: *Let me summarize for a minute. Both of you were really pleased to be part of the team, and to be working on the Auto Universe project. But each of you had a different idea about how the project would proceed. So let's look at some of the concerns you mentioned that have kept the project from meeting its goal. You both mentioned physical space and communication modes, including e-mails and phone calls. All of these involve personal boundaries in one form or another. Let's talk about each of them one at a time. First, physical space—the personal space around your desks. One of the concerns seems to be about what is put on the cubicle wall that is adjacent to both of your desks. Let's discuss this concern that you both mentioned.*

Trisha: *I believe that common spaces are supposed to be kind of neutral, you know—that we shouldn't have a lot of personal things in them. I feel embarrassed by some of the pictures and decorations that Vivian puts up; you know, there she is with her boyfriend at the beach.*

Pedro: *Vivian, what about you?*

Vivian: *Look, I had no idea that this bothered you so much. I get inspired by seeing happy times—and with the computer and other office stuff covering so much of the space in the cubicle, there's no real room for the pictures on my private part of the cubicle. I wasn't trying to tick you off. You never even brought it up to me before—that's what's weird to me.*

Pedro: *It's clear that the two of you are inspired in very different ways in order to do your best work. And it's important that both of you bring your best to your jobs.*

Vivian: *Hey, listen, I could buy one of those electronic photo things to put on my desk—you know, the kind that changes photos every few seconds. That could work if it really is a problem for you....*

Pedro: *Thank you, Vivian for already coming up with ideas to help resolve the situation. In a few minutes we'll come back to that. But now we're still making sure we're on the same page. One thing that you mentioned, Vivian, is your concern about the lack of communication regarding the issue. Let's focus on communication and each of your expectations around communicating with your coworker before we go any further ...*

Conflict #2: Manners or Meanness? (one employee accuses the other of treating her rudely)

Norita *(summarizing the icebreaker): I think it's interesting that all three of us are very competitive. I took this position in order to make our division the most successful one in the company. Patty, you were eager to take on the challenge of making the administrative tasks run as smoothly and hassle-free as possible. And Tom, you've been working your tail off to beat the other sales reps.*

All three of us are also used to being recognized for our achievements, and when we aren't, it bothers us. Let's talk for a minute about how this situation has affected each of you, and on the company as a whole.

Norita (a few minutes later, after some discussion): *Patty, I want to make sure you heard that Tom never intended to be rude. (Patty nods.) All right, good. And Tom, you've said you can be brusque to people in the office when you're feeling stressed, especially after spending all day bending over backward for customers. But do you hear that Patty wants—and deserves—the same respect that any customer would get?*

(Tom nods emphatically.) *Good. What's most important here is that, for both of you, the impact of what happened was not what you intended. Are we all on the same page? Okay, then, let's talk a bit about the incident last Friday when Tom tried to start a conversation with Patty...*

Conflict #3: Don't Shift on Me (a simmering conflict between two nursing supervisors over a new computerized tracking system and employee loyalty)

Maryanne *opens the meeting: I'm glad you were both able to arrange your schedules to be here today. We have several important things to talk about, including the new tracking system, adequate staffing on each of your shifts, and the general morale of the department. We'll get to those in a minute—but, first, I want to set a different tone from what's been happening. You are both extremely effective supervisors. Each of you is a large part of why the labor and delivery department of this hospital has such a good reputation. I don't want to lose that. It's also clear that you have very different management styles. I'm curious about how each of you got inspired to go into nursing. In my case, it was because both my parents were nurses. Both took great pride in their work, and they would show me thank-you letters they got from some of the patients they cared for. Norma, who was your mentor or role model when you began your nursing career?*

Norma speaks briefly about her aunt, who recently passed away from breast cancer—and who had inspired her to go into medicine instead of social work.

Maryanne *then turns to Danelle. And you, Danelle? Who inspired you?*

Danelle talks about her older sister's very difficult experience with multiple pregnancies and about why she decided to go into women's health.

Maryanne concludes the icebreaker by saying:

So we've each been influenced by an important family member. It also seems as if both of you have a special mission involving women. And yet, that mission may be derailed if we don't deal with the situation between the two of you. You should each know that I've had to spend time responding to complaints and gossip about how the two of you treat each other. Clearly, the issue is affecting the entire department. It's got to be hard on each of you as well. How has it affected you, Danelle?

After a brief exchange of how the situation has impacted each of them, Maryanne moves to one of the other issues on her issue list: what the two supervisors need from each other in order to keep things running smoothly.

Conflict #4: Who Gets the Job? (the promotion of a relative newcomer over a talented company veteran)

By the time Simon comes to the joint meeting, he seems relaxed and almost happy. It quickly becomes clear that he has thought long and hard about his future in the company. He has concluded that he doesn't want to leave the company, the metro area, or his current job. Mike, too, has thought about how important Simon would be to the department, and wants to find a way to keep him—and to get along with him.

After some preliminary welcoming remarks, Brad begins the icebreaker by saying:

Before we dive in, let's all brag for a moment. I'd like to hear about a professional accomplishment that each of you is proud of.

For example, I don't know if either of you knows this, but before I came here I worked for the state government for 11 years. I was given a citation signed by the governor for my performance, and I even won a couple of awards for innovation.

Mike, you're a relative newcomer to this company, but not to the field. You've been around and done a lot. Please tell us a little about one of your biggest accomplishments before you got here.

After Mike tells his success story, it's Simon's turn. But for Simon, Brad phrases the question differently:

> *Simon, you've been here for 15 years. You've seen this organization grow from a mom-and–pop operation to a 100-person business. Tell us about a specific project that you were part of that really moved the company forward in a big way.*

Brad summarizes by saying:

> *You've both made significant contributions to the field. And if we can get beyond the issue of who got the promotion and why, it looks to me like both of you will keep making important contributions, both to Sun Systems and to the whole industry.*

He then moves to a discussion of impact:

> *I know it hasn't been easy these last few weeks since the decision was announced. I'd like to hear how each of you expected the other to react to the announcement. Let's start with you, Mike. How did you think Simon would react?*

Both Mike and Simon speak about their expectations for how the other might have reacted. Brad then asks each of them, one at a time, to compare the other person's expectations with how they actually did react. Brad realizes that both employees are now ready to move on to the issues themselves.

7

Problem Solving: Building a Solution Together

Criticism has the power to do good when there is something that must be destroyed, dissolved or reduced; but [it is] capable only of harm when there is something to be built.

—Carl Jung

You are now ready for Stage IV of The Exchange: problem solving. This stage takes place during the joint meeting and flows directly out of the clarifying conversation, that is, Stage III.

Stage IV involves building a solution together. You and your employees are now a team, collaborating to create what will work best for the situation. All of you will do this one layer or issue at a time. At this point, you are not only facilitating the discussion; you are also encouraging the employees to come up with workable solutions.

Throughout this stage, remember to stay relaxed and open, and to speak calmly and cordially. You want your employees to feel that the meeting is a safe place to examine and explore possibilities. If people become afraid that their ideas will be immediately rejected or subjected to critical scrutiny, they will be reluctant to offer suggestions, especially creative ones. The goal here is to build, not destroy—and, as Jung noted, the surest way to destroy is through criticism. The surest way to build, however, is through encouragement.

We don't mean to imply that there will not be objective measures by which to judge each solution—but these will come later, after the ideas have flowed freely.

Stage IV is partly a brainstorming session. This means not hurrying things and not pressuring people. Paradoxically, the more you try to hurry things along, the more nervous people will get, and the slower everything will go. Of course, some situations don't need a lot of time or discussion. If a solution has become evident to everyone, by all means adopt it promptly.

Once people get to this point in The Exchange, they are usually willing to find workable solutions. You may be surprised at how efficient and effective this part of the process is, especially when you are truly open to employees' ideas and don't try to force one particular solution.

By now, you may have some good ideas of your own about how to resolve the situation. *Hold onto those ideas*; don't share them yet. For your employees to believe that their input matters, they need to be listened to, and they need to have their suggestions taken seriously. If you start by making suggestions of your own too early, even good ones, most employees will simply agree to whatever you suggest, and the entire process will come to a halt. You are their superior, so they're not going to compete with you. The meeting will then end quickly, and little or nothing will change. Worse, both employees will conclude that the failure to resolve the conflict is *your* fault, and the whole process will be dismissed as a waste of time.

Nevertheless, your input is extremely valuable. You may be able to deal with some aspects of the situation that they cannot. So, stay engaged in the process of looking for solutions—and also demonstrate your willingness to help improve the situation. It is a balance between encouraging your employees to find solutions while also looking for workable solutions yourself.

Begin by inviting suggestions. Ask open-ended questions that encourage people to talk. Some examples:

- *What suggestions do each of you have for resolving this?*
- *How would you like to see this situation dealt with?*
- *What would be some solutions that might satisfy everyone?*

As people offer ideas, it's important that you not criticize, evaluate, or comment on them. In fact, you shouldn't react to them at all. Just jot them down, and make it clear that you've heard and noted each suggestion. Some people paraphrase or repeat what they've heard and ask to make sure that they've captured the essence of each idea.

People usually begin by proposing obvious and conventional solutions. These probably won't work; if they did, your employees would have already used them. Nevertheless, let these ideas flow. After a few minutes, though, encourage your employees to think differently by saying something similar to this:

- *What else might work? Don't be afraid to suggest something unusual or strange. Even if it sounds crazy at first, there may be pieces of it that we can use or adapt.*
- *Is there some other approach to this situation that's beginning to form in your mind?*
- *If we tried a solution that's completely new and different, what might it look like?*

You can also encourage people individually. For example: *Harriet, you look thoughtful. Is an idea coming together for you?*

Give people time to think, and reassure them that a few minutes of silent contemplation is okay.

As people offer ideas, don't rush into discussing them. Instead, remind them that you're just gathering ideas right now; the three of you will discuss, evaluate, and select from the possible solutions in a few minutes.

If both people seize on an idea and want to work with it, make it clear that this will be the first idea you'll consider together once all the options are on the table.

Keep brainstorming and writing down possible solutions until people run dry.

At this point it's okay to offer ideas of your own, especially those that make sure your organization's interests are addressed.

Again, presenting ideas as open-ended questions can work wonders. For example:

- *What might happen if we held a meeting of everyone just to talk about deadlines?*
- *Are there subjects that you think would be better addressed in person, rather than by e-mail?*
- *What if the company offered people earbuds for listening to music while they worked?*
- *Do you think it would help if the Selection Committee sent all employees a memo explaining their decision and acknowledging the skills and talents of both finalists?*

You now have a list of choices. The next task is to select the most appropriate ones.

Sometimes the best choice or choices will be clear to everyone. In other situations, people will see that the whole conflict was a simple misunderstanding. In either of these cases, don't belabor things. Say something like this: *My understanding is that we've agreed on a solution, which is _____. Is that how both of you see it?*

In some cases, however, things won't be this easy. The three of you will need to discuss and consider a variety of suggestions, select one, and perhaps modify it to make it acceptable. Or, you may need to combine several ideas into one. The three of you may decide to try a solution temporarily and evaluate it after a trial period. (In such a case, set up a meeting later on for the three of you to review the situation and decide on the next steps.)

Be clear about your expectations. Remember that this is a three-way conversation that includes you. Although you want to encourage full participation in problem solving with your employees, you will also add your own suggestions. You will probably need to reject some options. You don't leave your manager hat at the door when you facilitate this discussion; you simply add additional skills and techniques to manage a difficult situation.

In some cases, creating a solution together will require a good deal of patience and effort from everyone. This is often the case when:

- A solution requires people to change how they act.
- The conflict is very personal.
- The dispute involves cultural issues.
- The central issue is about values.
- The dispute has no simple or clear-cut solution.

You'll remember from earlier in this book that unspoken interests, hopes, and needs underlie almost every dispute. When no clear solution emerges, focusing on people's interests can often create a breakthrough. As we discussed in Chapter 4, the primary interests employees have are

- Having their input valued
- Autonomy
- Fairness
- Acceptance
- Getting a chance to succeed
- Being treated respectfully

You can often encourage a solution by asking people to focus on one or more of their interests. For example, here's how the discussions about solutions might begin in each of our four sample scenarios:

> *(The Space Race) We need to keep our department productive, and at the same time we need to allow each of you some flexibility with your very different work styles, so that both of you will be satisfied and productive.*
>
> *(Manners or Meanness) It's important that all of us respect each other—and that we continuously demonstrate that respect. We also need to check with each other if something doesn't seem right. If you're not feeling respected, you need to be able to say, "Hey, did I do something to tick you off?" And if you're the person being asked that question, you need to say either, "Yeah, you did; here's why I'm upset" or "No, not at all; I'm sorry—it's not about you."*
>
> *(Don't Shift on Me) You're both obviously concerned about fairness, and so am I. What can we do about the staffing situation to make it fair to everyone, while making sure that we have enough good people on every shift?*
>
> *(Who Gets the Job) We need to let Mike lead, since that's his job. But Simon also needs to be recognized for his important contributions over the years. And people throughout the organization need to know that loyalty and longevity count.*

This approach enables people to focus on the human aspects of any solution rather than just its technical and logistical aspects. It also demonstrates that you want your employees' needs to get addressed.

Here are some other useful tips for building positive solutions:

- Use and encourage positive language. Solutions should focus on what people *will* do, not on what they won't or can't do.
- Use plain English, not bureaucratese.
- Use people's names, not their roles.
- Use the present tense and active verbs. For example, say (or write), *Tom, you agree to be respectful and courteous to other employees* rather than *Going forward, courteousness shall be demonstrated in all situations.*
- Use incentives, not punishments.
- As you craft solutions, make sure that each one is SMART:

- **Specific**—Be clear about who will do what, when, where, and how.
- **Measurable**—Be clear about how you will all be able to tell that something has been done, achieved, or completed.
- **Achievable**—Make sure that whatever solution you agree on fits the situation; that it complies with both the law and organizational policy; and that everyone involved has the ability and opportunity to do what is required of them. Don't set up anyone to fail.
- **Realistic**—Check calendar dates for holidays and vacations; look at past performance to predict future actions; allow extra time for glitches and delays; don't assume that the best-case scenarios will come true.
- **Timed**—Create reasonable deadlines or target dates; include a few ideas about what to do if something unexpected occurs; be willing to set new dates if necessary.

Once the three of you have settled on some workable solutions, write them down. This shouldn't be a formal contract—a few notes to yourself are sufficient for the moment.

Do, however, put the agreed-upon solutions in writing as soon as possible. If you're in a room with a computer, type a memo or e-mail to both people while both of them look over your shoulder. Make sure that your wording satisfies them both. Alternatively, send both people a memo or e-mail as soon as possible after the meeting, and ask each one to confirm that it contains their agreed-upon solutions.

Putting solutions in writing is very important, and not just for legal reasons (and for covering your back). It's a way to honor the work that the three of you accomplished. It's also a way to keep people's memories from diverging from the agreed-upon solutions. Verbal agreements have a way of being remembered very differently by different people—and then becoming the subject of another conflict. It's safer and easier for everyone to have the solutions written down, in order to be able to easily verify them later.

Let both employees know that this written agreement is not a legal contract, a performance appraisal, or a written warning. Also assure them that the document won't be put in their personnel file. However if, for some unusual reason, the agreement *does* need to go in an employee's personnel file, tell them so. Also have them sign it, and give them a photocopy.

After the meeting is over, both employees will return to their work-spaces, where their colleagues will expect them to convey what happened. Meanwhile, you will still be a manager tomorrow, and your employees will be watching you. Thus, it's important for all three of you to report to your colleagues that you've gained something, and that the process you went through together worked well.

With this in mind, end The Exchange by coming to a clear agreement about what all of you will say about the meeting. This is important because you want all employees to hear the same version of what happened in your joint session.

This does *not* mean you have to tell all; it just means that the three of you will create a common, accurate, and well-considered message about the meeting and its results. This might be a simple, informal statement such as: *Julia, Spencer, and Owen spent some time talking and decided that they would all consult with each other before making any further changes to the project.* Or, one of you might write a group e-mail or memo explaining what happened in the meeting; once the other two have reviewed and approved it, it will go out to multiple people.

Some employees may want only certain aspects of the meeting to be shared, such as those matters that affect everyone or have to do with a particular policy. Some folks may want to keep their personal agreements private. That's fine. The most important concern is that the three of you together decide exactly what will and will not be shared with other employees.

USING THE EXCHANGE: BUILDING A SOLUTION TOGETHER

Conflict #1: The Space Race (two programmers on a project team work in adjacent cubicles—and get on each other's nerves)

- Pedro agrees to provide earbuds for anyone on the team who requests them.
- Vivian agrees to purchase an electronic photo stand for her desk and to remove the photos on the shared cubicle wall. She will do both of these by next Monday morning.
- Vivian agrees to make all her personal conversations and phone calls during her breaks in the employee lounge.
- Trisha and Vivian agree to copy each other on all e-mails regarding the Auto Universe project.
- Trisha and Vivian agree to meet once every 2 weeks to discuss the programming that they are working on and address any concerns that may have arisen.
- Both agree to go out for coffee together at the corner café on Monday after their first meeting.

Conflict #2: Manners or Meanness? (one employee accuses the other of treating her rudely)

- Norita agrees to hold a half-day staff retreat in place of the next scheduled monthly staff meeting, so employees can become more familiar and comfortable with each other.
- Tom and Patty apologize to each other. Both commit to talking directly to each other when either feels offended, mistreated, or ignored by the other.
- Tom also agrees that when he feels especially pressured and overwhelmed, he will text Patty a message that will express his frustration at his customers. Patty agrees to text back to commiserate with Tom when she can.

Conflict #3: Don't Shift on Me (a simmering conflict between two nursing supervisors over a new computerized patient tracking system and employee loyalty)

- Norma and Danelle agree to hold joint interviews with the nurses who requested transfers, to learn more about their needs and concerns.

- They agree to develop some standard protocols about work standards, which will be posted in each nurses' station.
- All three women agree to hold a joint meeting during each shift to talk about the new patient tracking system. All three will be present at each meeting to convey unity and support for the system.
- Maryanne agrees to ask that a computer specialist from the IT Department offer seminars at the hospital about the new patient tracking system, and to provide individual tutoring for anyone who asks for it.

Conflict #4: Who Gets the Job? (the promotion of a relative newcomer over a talented company veteran)

- Mike and Simon agree to a restructuring of the department that will give Simon more responsibility and make him eligible for a bigger raise next year.
- Brad agrees to propose to HR that when any future vacancy occurs, a clear statement of selection criteria will be posted on the company's intranet site, along with the vacancy notice.
- Mike, Simon, and Brad agree to tell anyone who asks that they had "a constructive discussion and will be planning to do a joint presentation soon about a new idea for structuring the department."
- If pressed about Mike's promotion, all agree to say, "We've agreed to go with the present situation and support the goals of the department."
- Brad tells the CEO that the situation has been resolved.

8

Culture, Diversity, and Other Things That Matter

It is not our purpose to become each other; it is to recognize each other, to learn to see the other and honor him for what he is.

—Hermann Hesse

Hermann Hesse probably knew we couldn't become each other even if we wanted to, because we are separated by culture.

Culture is a contributing cause to almost every conflict. Cultural concerns can be very helpful in resolving disputes—and instrumental in creating disasters if they are ignored.

We define *culture* as the way things are done in a particular group. A culture is rooted in values about people's places in society, how they view authority, how they think, and how they communicate.

Every society, workplace, industry, organization, and family has its own unique culture. This culture dictates all kinds of individual and collective behaviors. For example, in some organizations it's fine to take a coffee break that lasts more than 15 minutes, while in others it's considered a clear flouting of the rules. In some organizations, 8 a.m. means 8:00 a.m.—not 8:05, or even 8:02; at others, it means between 8 and 8:15.

Language is always a part of culture. As negotiator Raymond Cohen has observed, "Language is not a neutral, transparent window through which the world reveals itself. Rather, it is a culturally charged set of symbols for representing the world." The same words often mean different things to different people. Differences in national origin, gender, education, race, and profession often result in people hearing the same words in very different ways.

This is especially true for second-language speakers. For example, a German businessman working in the rural United States repeatedly referred to his company's customers as "peasants." Not surprisingly, customers complained that he looked down on them, and some of his colleagues refused to work with him. However, when a young college intern who spoke German joined the team, it took him only a day to realize that his German colleague wasn't being snobbish. The German term *der bauer* can be translated as either "farmer" or "peasant," and the businessman thought that the two words had identical meanings. He had no idea that he was insulting people; he thought he was just being accurate. When the intern pointed out his mistake to him, he was surprised and embarrassed. He promptly explained and apologized for his error to his colleagues. The entire conflict, which had been steadily escalating, quickly vanished.

Similar misunderstandings can occur across industries, when (for example) a common word or phrase has a particular meaning in one industry, and a very different meaning in another. (For example, a professional stripper works with photographic negatives. Another kind of professional stripper may pose nude for some of those photographs.)

The same kind of misunderstanding can also occur between members of different professions *within the same industry*. It's very common to find that employees who work at a one level view other employees at a different level as if they were aliens.

The healthcare industry is a perfect example. Even though doctors and nurses often use the same words, they are trained to use those words differently. Nurses are trained to look at the whole patient, while doctors are trained to look at specific symptoms in order to diagnose particular maladies. As a result, different reactions and very different treatments can result when a health care professional says in the middle of the night, "The patient is very uncomfortable." A physician who speaks these words may be saying that the patient has a symptom that should be dealt with in the morning. The nurse, however, may be calling for immediate intervention. It's no wonder that, in health care, communication failures are often causes of unintentional patient harm.

Indeed, the simple word *yes* can lead to a whole range of misunderstandings. We use it primarily to communicate our agreement. However, some people also say yes just to politely acknowledge that they've heard the speaker; they understand but don't necessarily agree. Still others say yes when they mean, "Go on; tell me more."

When Americans communicate with people from some Asian countries, the opportunities for misunderstandings are manifold. In Japan, for example, it's traditionally been considered rude to overtly say no. Instead of saying, *No, I can't take on another assignment of that size*, someone from Japan might say, *Perhaps one of my colleagues would be more appropriate.* To an American, this can sound like passive/aggressive behavior, laziness, or an attempt to shirk responsibility.

There are also subcultures within the United States that train their members to be indirect—some very religious communities, for example, where intragroup harmony is one of the most important values.

Reluctance to say no is also common when employees feel the person they're communicating with has much more power. They may think that they do not have the right to say no. Instead, they may use coded sentences such as *That might be difficult.* (This is when you will need to say something like, *I'm hearing that you don't think this is a good idea. Fair enough. What do you suggest instead?*)

In some cultures, indirection goes well beyond avoiding the word *no*. In some Asian and African cultures, for example, people rarely say *anything* directly; they drop hints and expect others to get the message. It's considered impolite to ask for things; having to ask also creates a loss of face. It's okay to hint, however. It's up to the other person to understand the hint and to respond to the implied request without being overtly asked.

When direct communicators (such as most Americans, Latinos, and Europeans) work together with indirect communicators, the differences in their communication styles can easily create conflicts. The indirect folks may consider the direct ones to be rude, bombastic, and obtuse, while the direct folks may see the indirect ones as evasive, wishy-washy, or uncommunicative.

People from both types of cultures almost always think they are communicating clearly. And they *are*—when speaking with other members of their own groups. But they aren't communicating clearly if the conversation is cross-cultural.

The best way to know that the message you sent is the one that was received is to talk about it when you observe a reaction that's different from the one you expected.

Then, there is the issue of volume. Most people generally speak at a decibel level that they've learned is most effective. However, most of us also raise our voices when we want to add emphasis—or when we're excited, angry, or enthusiastic. This means that when we speak loudly, people can infer a wide range of things—most of them inaccurate—about why we're being loud.

Finally, there is the practice of interrupting someone while they speak. Some cultures (and some families and individuals) view any interruption to a speaker as rude. Others interrupt occasionally as a form of politeness, to show that they're paying close attention, and to express their passion and appreciation for the speaker's words. When these people talk, if there are no interruptions, they may assume that others are indifferent, bored, or dismissive.

Thus, depending on whom you speak with, an interruption may be considered rude—or *not* interrupting occasionally might be considered rude. This is how people come to conclusions such as *she never listens* or *he doesn't care about the project at all.*

Of course, there is a great deal more to communication than the words people say and the way they say them. Linguists have noted that in most conversations including emotional issues only 7% of the message a listener hears is conveyed in the actual words. Tone of voice accounts for 38%, and body language accounts for 55%. So, while it's important to use words carefully, it's equally important to be aware of tone and body language, especially when we communicate with people from other cultures. Let us look at some important aspects of this nonverbal communication.

> **Eye contact.** In some Western cultures, making direct eye contact is interpreted as a sign of honesty, respect, and straightforwardness. In other cultures, however, direct eye contact, especially with people in higher positions, is considered rude or challenging. As you use The Exchange and meet with people, offer them the opportunity for eye contact, at least occasionally. If they avoid your eyes, however, don't try to force them to look you in the face.

> **Personal space.** The amount of personal space someone needs around their body is both personally and culturally determined. Americans often need the most; we generally stand about a foot and a half away from friends and family, and 2 feet (or more) away from colleagues and strangers. Whatever the size of someone's comfort zone, when someone else enters it, the person may feel threatened, harassed, or even in danger. If, as you conduct The Exchange, someone seems intensely uncomfortable, try increasing the amount of personal space around them, and see if they relax.

Gestures. Some cultures encourage broad, sweeping hand, or arm movements; others use more closed gestures and subtle shakes of the head to communicate meanings. Someone from Italy, for example, may interpret the subdued smile of their Indian colleague as a lack of interest, when in fact she is fascinated—and, from her viewpoint, expressing that fascination.

Thinking styles. Even the way in which people think about work tasks can differ widely from person to person. Some people are sequential thinkers; others are all-at-once thinkers. Some employees quickly grasp a complicated concept and can do several tasks simultaneously. Others can do their work very well but need to focus on one assignment at a time.

When a multitasker and a single-focus person work together on a project, their different approaches to work can sometimes create conflicts. The single-tasker may see the multitasker as indifferent or not paying attention, while the multitasker may see the single-tasker as rigid and uncreative—and, perhaps, not terribly bright.

TIPS FOR BRIDGING CULTURAL GAPS

- Pick out specific words that are involved in the conflict, such as *the project, deadlines,* and *personal calls.* Ask each person to define each term for the other. This may reveal how some miscommunication may have occurred.
- When everyone seems to be saying yes to an idea or proposal, ask each person—in a sincere, curious, nonpedantic tone—to summarize what they understand the proposal to be.
- Describe aloud the body language and eye contact of each employee. Then ask each person to talk briefly about how the other's nonverbal communication affects them. If a gesture or action has been misinterpreted, give the employee in question a chance to briefly explain what they meant by that gesture or action. For example: *I noticed, Bob, that when you raised your voice just now, Cindy flinched. Cindy, what did you think Bob was conveying?* Then check with Bob to see if he was really understood. Cindy may have thought he was angry when he was merely emphasizing a point.

- If you think an employee is missing the other person's point, ask them to recap or summarize the other's message. Soon afterward, ask the second employee to recap or summarize something the first one says, so that neither employee feels singled out.
- Watch each person's reactions. If you see something that you were not expecting (a change in how someone is sitting, for example, or a sudden reluctance to speak when it is clearly a time for them to do so), ask the person about it. *Salim, I saw that you've moved to the edge of your seat—is there someone I forgot to mention? Or, Nadia, I notice that you're really quiet all of a sudden. Did I say something that didn't sit right with you? It's very important that this agreement reflect everyone's needs, and I want to make sure you have a say in it.*

THE ROLE OF CULTURE IN FOUR CONFLICTS

Conflict #1: The Space Race (two programmers on a project team work in adjacent cubicles—and get on each other's nerves)

Vivian and Trisha have very different perceptions about what constitutes personal space. Vivian comes from an informal culture where the group is considered more important than its individual members. To Vivian, calls from her large extended family are not personal in the same way that a friend's call would be. She didn't understand how or why these calls might irritate a coworker. Also, she is accustomed to having family pictures everywhere in her home, so having personal pictures at work seemed perfectly natural to her. In contrast, Trisha is an only child whose culture focused on individual achievement. She was taught that only business calls are appropriate in a workplace.

Vivian is used to many people living in close quarters, so she is perfectly comfortable with just inches separating her from her coworker. Trisha, who grew up with her own room in a large house, feels almost physically threatened by Vivian's physical proximity.

Pedro asks Vivian and Trisha to each explain exactly what kind of personal space and boundaries they need in order to do their job well. After they both answer his question, they both begin to understand the source of the conflict.

Conflict #2: Manners or Meanness? (one employee accuses the other of treating her rudely)

Patty is an indirect communicator; Tom is as direct as anyone can be. When Tom was brusque with Patty, she felt he was indirectly showing condescension and disrespect. Yet, as an indirect communicator, she was unwilling to challenge Tom about his behavior. So, instead, she indirectly communicated her own displeasure with him, by not making eye contact with him and turning away when he came into the room. Patty thought it should be obvious to Tom that he had hurt her feelings.

Tom could tell that Patty was upset with him, but he had no idea why, and he was oblivious to the impact he was having on her. Furthermore, as a direct communicator, he assumed that if Patty wanted him to act differently, she would tell him. But to Tom, being brusque and super-direct, just meant he was frazzled or busy; he didn't think anyone would take it personally.

Norita doesn't want to lose either employee. She helps Tom and Patty to work out a set of steps Patty can take if and when she feels disregarded in the future. Tom, in turn, agrees to ask Patty if something is wrong whenever she seems troubled. Patty also agrees to practice being more direct with him.

Conflict #3: Don't Shift on Me (a simmering conflict between two nursing supervisors over a new computerized patient tracking system and employee loyalty)

Danelle is a multitasker who often works on several projects at a time. She likes to have materials for each project visible, so there are lots of piles on her desk when she is on duty. Danelle sometimes answers the phone or talks briefly with other people while in the middle of a conversation.

Norma prefers a filing system with one file open at a time. She has her to-do lists and likes to check off one task at a time. *A time for everything* is her motto, and she usually finishes one project before beginning another. Norma doesn't like to be interrupted when she is concentrating.

Using The Exchange, Maryanne is able to get each supervisor to talk about her style and her needs. A breakthrough occurs when each woman is able to describe the benefits of the other's style without adding a comment about what is wrong with it.

Conflict #4: Who Gets the Job? (the promotion of a relative newcomer over a talented company veteran)

Mike, the newly promoted operations supervisor, was recruited, and then promoted, to change the company's rather quiet, lax, laid-back culture. Mike is hardworking, energetic, articulate, and charismatic. Simon is a much slower and more thoughtful speaker. He's very smart and creative, and almost everyone likes him, but nobody sees him as inspiring or a strong leader.

There was no question that Mike had much more leadership potential. But, because the selection process was opaque, many employees, including Simon, felt disrespected, ignored, and unappreciated.

Brad asked each employee to describe the qualities important for leading the department. Under Brad's guidance, the list grew to be quite extensive and included the ability to give directions, supervising and giving feedback to other employees, schmoozing with potential buyers, and attending endless, boring meetings of the company's executive team. It soon became very clear that Simon hated that constant exposure to other people, while Mike reveled in it. Understanding this difference in how each man was comfortable in a leadership role, helped each other to see each other in a different light.

The real breakthrough, however, came when Brad agreed to push for a set of criteria for promotions that would create transparency in future hiring, satisfying an agency-wide desire for more openness.

9

Making the Most of The Exchange in Your Organization

> Without change, there are no breakthroughs, and without breakthroughs, there is no future.
>
> **—Anonymous adage on a plaque**

Up to this point, we have talked about The Exchange in terms of three people—you and two employees who are in conflict. However, sometimes conflicts involve more than two key people—for example, an entire department can be in conflict. And sometimes *you* may be part of the conflict.

The Exchange can be adapted for these situations, as well as many others. It's even a useful way to make collaborative decisions and achieve breakthroughs when there is no conflict at all.

In all of these situations, The Exchange offers an alternative to the way things are traditionally resolved or, all too often, left unresolved. In this chapter, we'll describe several useful variations on the basic model of The Exchange.

USING THE EXCHANGE FOR A GROUP CONFLICT

Sometimes a conflict involves multiple employees. Some examples:

- Because of a dramatic and organization-wide policy change in a large corporation, 8500 employees have separated into two camps: the resisters, who support the tried-and-true ways that have always worked, and the innovators, who actively welcome change and are eager to do better than the status quo. Eight top executives of the corporation have emerged as spokespeople—four for each point of view.
- In the wake of a merger of two large nonprofits, one group of employees views another group as outsiders; the outsiders, in turn, see the other group as a clique of turf-protecting snobs.
- One department in a Fortune 1000 corporation becomes pitted against another for recognition, resources, and/or power.
- For the past 25 years, a division of a midsize private company has functioned well. Throughout this time, employees had clear job descriptions, and each worked on their own particular project or assignment, consulting others as needed. Now, however, the company has a new president, who insists on creating a project-oriented, team-based culture.
- The ten members of a research department in a small private university are embroiled in a destructive conflict over who gets credit (and who doesn't) when publishing their findings in an academic journal. Politics, seniority, and complaints about gender bias all rear their heads. Eventually the teaching assistants are affected by the venom being spewed.

In some cases, the situations described earlier may require professional mediators. On the other hand, if you have the appropriate role in one of these organizations, the respect of the people involved, and experience in dealing with complex conflicts, you may be able to use The Exchange to create a successful resolution.

For any such conflict, you will need to do some initial analysis and investigation. You will also need to approach the situation strategically. Your joint session may include several (or many) people, so plan for that session to take more time than it would if only two employees were involved. A session of 60–90 minutes is typical. And when there are not only a lot of people but complex issues, it's not unusual to need several joint sessions to work through Phases III and IV. (But you may also be amazed at how efficiently a large joint meeting can flow.)

Here's a more detailed breakdown of how to adapt The Exchange for group conflicts.

STAGE I: HOLD PRIVATE MEETINGS

Yes, you will still have private meetings—but not with every affected employee.

There are two general approaches to holding private meetings when working with groups. One approach is to arrange a private meeting with a key person—or a few key people—from each unit, group, or camp. Pick people whom you feel will give you honest assessments of *each* side's interests. In most cases, this should result in no more than half a dozen private meetings.

Another option is to meet with *all* the people who hold a particular viewpoint, and then ask *them* to select one or two people to represent them at a joint meeting. The upside of this is that it creates a mini-democracy for each side. The downside is that either side may choose to be represented by someone who is especially contentious. You can help avoid this by encouraging each interest group to ask itself these questions when choosing its representative:

- Who do you trust to accurately represent your group?
- Who would the *other* side most trust, or at least believe?
- Who has the best communication skills?

Without such criteria, many groups may choose the staunchest or most argumentative representatives, not necessarily the most effective ones.

In both approaches, your private meetings begin with you explaining their purpose and describing your interests. You then ask people for their perspectives on the situation, and you listen carefully to their responses.

Next, give people a chance to get some of their volatile emotions out of the way, so that later, in the group meeting, issues can be discussed productively and the group session doesn't devolve into a loud free-for-all. Just as in one-on-one private meetings, take a few minutes to let people express their feelings. When you hear the same words being used again and again, however, it's time to move on. Acknowledge the depth of people's feelings, but say that in the joint session to follow, the goal will be a resolution of the conflict, not a rehashing of events and grievances. You might say something like this:

It's clear that some of you have been deeply affected by this conflict, and it will be important for the other group to understand this. It's also clear that we all need to move beyond the past. Remember that our goal is to resolve the situation so that it won't continue to stand in the way of productivity. So, before the group meeting, think about what might be the best way to reach a resolution that will accomplish this.

It's also important to emphasize that the upcoming joint session will deal solely with group issues, not individual complaints.

STAGE II: DEVELOP AN ISSUE LIST

While it's always important to have an issue list for joint meetings, when you're dealing with groups it's absolutely critical.

An icebreaker is also especially helpful when a group session includes more than two employees, because it reminds everyone of life beyond the present conflict. In addition, it reminds the groups that they have some things in common, such as an interest in their jobs or a belief in the mission of the organization.

When you have six or more people sitting around a conference table, your icebreaker can easily take 10–15 minutes—but that's okay, because getting people to listen to each other and relax is extremely important to the success of The Exchange.

Here are some icebreakers that work very well with groups—and usually go fairly quickly:

- *What do you most value about working here?*
- *Tell us briefly about one of your most important professional successes or achievements.*
- *How did you come to work in this field?*
- *Tell us briefly about a talent or skill you have that most of us may not know about.*

If more than six people are in the room, your icebreaker will need to be designed so that employees can respond to it very briefly. For example:

- *I'd like each of you to say in ten words or less what motivates you to come to work each day.*
- *I'd like each person here to briefly describe three qualities of a well-functioning workplace.*
- *We're going to go around the room, and have everyone mention one project here that they're glad they worked on. Don't describe the project; just name it.*

In group conflicts, the main impact is on the group rather than on each individual. The conversation about impact will thus need to focus on the major issues affecting the unit, group, or camp, not on individual complaints.

To begin discussing this impact, you might ask questions such as these:

- *How is this issue affecting the department or group?*
- *Has it become harder for people to do their jobs and meet their targets? How? Why?*
- *What did people expect when things first started to change? How did these expectations differ from the reality?*

STAGE III: CONDUCT THE JOINT MEETING

If your joint session will have more than five people, including you—and with most group conflicts, it will—you'll need to give everyone a few ground rules for the discussion. Explain that these will ensure that the session proceeds smoothly, that everyone gets a chance to offer input, and that all of you will finish within 60–90 minutes. Here are some ground rules we suggest:

- **No one speaks twice on a topic until everyone who wants to has had a chance to speak once.** Not everyone will have something new to say. This is also a good way to keep one or two people from dominating the discussion.
- **Let each speaker finish before anyone responds.**

Present these ground rules at the very beginning, as part of your introduction to the conversation—not after someone has spoken, when it will seem as if that person did something wrong and you are correcting them. If you like, before the joint session begins, write the ground rules on a whiteboard or a sheet of posted flip-chart paper.

As you discuss impact and issues, it's important to minimize repetitions. One easy way to do this is to say, after each speaker has finished, *Does anyone have a different way of looking at the situation?* or *Is there anything new someone wants to add that hasn't been said yet?*

As the facilitator of the discussion, make sure that everyone has a chance to speak and is not deferring to others because of shyness or organizational status.

STAGE IV: BUILDING A SOLUTION TOGETHER

This stage of The Exchange can also be an opportunity for team-building. Your employees will have a meaningful discussion with coworkers whom they may have formerly viewed as opponents or competitors. You may thus find the atmosphere in the office much more congenial after you use The Exchange a few times.

Near the end of the group session, everyone present will need to decide what message to give to the groups that are represented and how to deliver that message. This decision may take some time and deliberation. That's fine—and well worth the time and trouble. The people in the room will be expected to report to their constituents; if they don't all report exactly the same thing, a new conflict is inevitable.

ADAPTING THE EXCHANGE FOR DISRUPTIVE PEOPLE

We've all had to deal with disruptive people at work. You know who we mean: prickly people who always seem to be at the center of some disruption or argument or conflict. Often there's not really a conflict between them and other employees; they just create an atmosphere of conflict wherever they go.

These folks can spread unease and tension throughout a workplace. Other employees will do almost anything to avoid dealing with them. The results can include poor performance, missed deadlines, and low morale. Occasionally, their colleagues even abandon their jobs or go on "stress leave."

If you supervise one of these people, you know how difficult it is to deal with them. Nothing is ever their fault, yet they always seem to be at the center of discontent. At the same time, however, their skills may be essential to the success of your organization. Here is how you can adapt The Exchange for such a person.

First of all, don't start with a private meeting, which would likely create yet another conflict—in this case, between you and the employee. Instead, go straight to Stage II and create an issue list. This list may be long, which is fine. You (and many other people in your workplace) probably have a very good idea of just what those issues are. However, do remember to frame these issues using neutral, nonblaming language.

In creating this issues list, ask yourself these questions:

- What specific incidents have you observed?
- What specific incidents and/or actions have been reported?
- Why are you choosing to handle the situation now?

Now consider the impact of the situation. Ask yourself these questions:

- What has been the employee's impact on others in the workplace? Are people making more mistakes? Missing deadlines? Calling in sick? Asking for transfers to other departments or locations?
- What might be the impact of *other people's* reactions on the problem employee? This will be an important question to ask in Stage III.

Then think about an icebreaker. This might be a compliment about one of the employee's recent accomplishments, or a question about their professional goals, or an acknowledgment of their completion of a difficult project or task.

Then think about what specific behavior changes you want from this person. Disruptive people are often completely unaware of the effect of their actions on others. They also may literally have no idea how to change their behavior—which may seem completely normal to them. You will want to keep in mind the changes you need the employee to make along with suggested behaviors during Stage IV, the problem-solving part of the meeting.

With a disruptive employee, you won't usually schedule a joint session with you, them, and a third party with whom they have a specific conflict.

For one thing, that third party could be almost anyone they work with. For another, in a standard three-person joint session they'll often create more conflict. Instead, Stages III and IV should take place in a two-person meeting of just you and them.

Call the employee and ask to meet with them for 60–90 minutes in your office or some other private space. Explain that the purpose of the meeting is to discuss some conflicts that have arisen, but don't mention any specific items on your issue list. As you make this request, use a neutral, cordial, nonanxious tone.

Begin your meeting by explaining the reasons for it and reviewing any confidentiality concerns (especially any exceptions to confidentiality and what will be placed in the employee's HR file). Briefly describe your own interests in resolving the issues. While it's important that neither of you views the meeting as a disciplinary session, tell the employee that, depending on what happens in the meeting, the next step may be the start of a discipline procedure.

Use your icebreaker, then briefly list the issues you want to address. When you have finished reading through these, ask the employee if they have any issues that they want to discuss. Add these to your list.

Next, ask the employee to briefly tell you how the situation has impacted them. For example:

> *Clearly, you have a passion for technology, and it seems that others' lack of knowledge has been frustrating for you. Can you talk a bit about how it is for you when you explain something several times to someone, and they still don't understand?*

After the employee has expressed their emotions—and you have acknowledged those emotions—begin talking about the impact the employee has had on other people in the workplace. You may want to explain how it has affected the overall morale or atmosphere, productivity, the quality of work or products, etc. Be as clear, specific, and concrete as you can about what you have observed.

You may also need to say clearly and firmly that these issues are not up for debate. So, for example, if your employee says, "Well, they shouldn't feel that way," you need to say firmly, "But they do, and that's part of what we're here to deal with."

Then go through the specific issues, one at a time. Get the employee to talk about each one. Ask what happened, and how what others did affected them. This is where respectful listening and responding can sometimes work wonders. After the employee has spoken, demonstrate that you have heard what they said, acknowledge the impacts of the situation on the employee, and ask open-ended questions to go deeper into the situation.

Remember, don't rush into problem solving until you are sure the employee really understands the effects of their actions and behavior on others.

When you do reach Stage IV, problem solving, it may be helpful for the two of you to address and create solutions for one behavior or recurring conflict at a time. As much as possible, include your employee's own ideas about what they are willing to do to make the situation better. Create a clear action plan with as many specifics as possible.

You will also need to be very clear about what will happen if things don't improve—for example, you might begin disciplinary procedures, or change their job assignment, or fire them. It's only fair that they know what the consequences of a particular action or refusal to act will be.

In some cases, you may be surprised to discover that a disruptive employee is actually relieved to be able to talk to someone who listens and treats them respectfully.

We know a physician who was stunned to discover that he was assisted by the same operating room nurse every time, not because she liked him, but because she was the only one willing to work with him. Only in an Exchange process, where he didn't lose face in front of others, could he look at his behavior in a different light. What he thought was simply being efficient in asking for instruments and handling the patient, the other nurses saw as bullying and overbearing.

In another situation, a manager used The Exchange with a high-potential employee who often made his coworkers angry. She decided to begin her meeting with a performance review. In preparing for the meeting, she realized that, in most aspects of his job, the employee had actually improved dramatically. She used this information as her icebreaker. Both people then felt so encouraged by these positive comments that they were able to focus on the problem areas without rancor.

Talking with disruptive or highly emotional employees isn't easy. However, The Exchange will help you *and* your employee deal respectfully—and more effectively—with conflicts, while enabling the employee to keep their dignity intact.

USING THE EXCHANGE WHEN YOU ARE SEEN AS PART OF THE PROBLEM

In every description of The Exchange thus far, you have not been a part of the conflict, and you have thus been able to maintain your emotional distance from it. The conflict may have affected you, but you were not at its center.

All of this changes when you are personally attacked or accused. For example:

- An employee accuses you of micromanaging her project.
- A long-time colleague suddenly turns on you, claiming that you are biased against him because of his age.
- You are on the receiving end of a tirade by one of your team leaders about unfair practices.

Suddenly, the emotional distance disappears—yet you need to put your ego aside and deal with the situation without reacting too emotionally.

If you are stuck in such a conflict, you can *still* use The Exchange to resolve it—especially if it is important to you that your employees trust you, or that you clear your name.

Using The Exchange in this situation is similar to using it with a disruptive person. One telling difference, however, is that your emotional reaction will probably be stronger because you are directly involved in the conflict. Thus, you will need to work harder to manage your reactions—and your own urge to become defensive.

In such a situation, you obviously can't be a completely neutral facilitator. You can, however, use key aspects of The Exchange to hold a single informal but structured meeting—presuming, of course, that you can get the other person in the conflict to meet with you.

It's generally a good idea to ask for this meeting as soon as possible after a conflict arises. This enables you to address the issue before it gets worse or bigger. It may also prevent formal complaints from becoming part of your employee record. In addition, it may save you hours of explaining yourself to other people in the organization.

Begin by inviting the other person in the conflict to meet with you one-to-one sometime soon, and agree on a time and place. Shortly before the meeting, take a few minutes to "meet with yourself" (in a modified Stage

II). Remind yourself that both you and the other person deserve respect. Review your own actions thus far and, if you think you have made a mistake, be ready to apologize. If you still think the other person is wrong, be prepared *not* to say so in your meeting—at least, not until you have heard their perspective.

If you can, create your own issue list before the two of you meet one to one. However, be prepared to revise the list based on new information you may hear from the other person. In your issue list, try to frame your concerns in language that won't inflame the situation—and won't imply that you know what the other person is thinking. So, for example, instead of writing "*You are sabotaging my work,*" write "*We appear to have different expectations about how we work together and what we need to deliver.*" Rather than writing "*I have heard rumors that you lied about me,*" write "*I want information about me and my intentions to be accurate.*" Instead of writing "*Stop micromanaging this project,*" write "*We need to have a smooth working relationship—and we need to keep the project on track.*"

Coming up with an icebreaker won't be hard; almost any of the examples in this book will work well. In this context, the icebreaker can be especially disarming. At the very least, it's a great opportunity to create a collegial tone and set the stage for cooperation.

You may need to make your best guesses about the impact and issues from the other person's viewpoint. Or you may create these from your own perspective, with the understanding that you may need to change them on the fly as your meeting proceeds.

At this one-to-one meeting, go informally through the four stages of The Exchange as best you can. Since you won't be acting as a formal facilitator, the meeting probably won't flow naturally from one stage to the next. That's okay. Listen carefully; speak calmly, cordially, and nonjudgmentally; don't criticize or pick apart the other person's thinking; and remember to transform positions into issues and emotions into impacts.

Begin with your icebreaker; then initiate the impact discussion by finding out what the situation looks like to the other person. Ask them how it affects them and their unit or group. Listen respectfully without commenting. Then acknowledge, summarize, and paraphrase their key points. Ask open-ended questions. This may be challenging because you may be tempted to defend yourself and explain your actions. Resist this temptation. The more you are able to withhold your reaction and let the person explain their own perspective, the better the session will go.

Once you have a good idea of the other person's perspective, *then* you can explain how the situation looks to you. Because you have shown that you understand by recapping the other person's key ideas, they may relax and be much more receptive to what you have to say.

Next, talk about how each of you reached the conclusions you did, and how you each came to your assumption about the other's intentions. Let the other person speak first. Remember, at this point, the goal is mutual understanding, not creating solutions. Focus on what actions led each of you to make the evaluations you did.

Now you are ready to propose, discuss, and select possible solutions. Brainstorm. Ask open-ended questions such as these:

- *Do you have some thoughts about how we can best deal with this?*
- *What would be a satisfactory way to resolve this?*
- *What do you most need in order to resolve this?*
- *Let us look beyond the standard solutions and ideas. What might work that other people might think of as strange or off the wall?*
- *What can we do to keep such conflicts from coming up again?*

Once the two of you have created a workable solution, don't forget to discuss and agree on an answer to this question: What should we tell people about this meeting when they ask?

USING THE EXCHANGE IN COLLABORATIVE DECISION MAKING

So far we have talked about using The Exchange to manage workplace conflicts. However, you can also use The Exchange to *prevent* honest disagreements from escalating into full-blown disputes.

Divergent views on interpreting policy, creating or implementing new policies, developing new programs, and building consensus on strategic plans—all of these situations are good opportunities for using The Exchange to make group decisions. The Exchange will help stimulate useful discussion, create buy-in, and dissolve knee-jerk resistance.

The Exchange is also a good way to perform reality tests on suggestions. For example, you might raise questions such as these:

- *What would that decision or focus look like? What would people do to carry it out?*
- *What steps would we have to take before that could happen?*
- *How likely is it that the others will buy into what you're proposing?*

It can be used to develop new procedures:

- *Could we achieve better results by doing it differently? In what ways?*
- *What steps do you see are needed for this to work? Which ones can we ignore or bypass?*

It is also a good way to develop the best route to new organizational destinations:

- *How do you see this fitting with the new directive?*
- *What do you see as the first step?*

In these situations, you'll focus on a new idea rather than a conflict, but you'll use the same tools and processes to collect people's impressions, forge agreements, and create solutions. You can also use many of the tools of The Exchange to keep meetings focused and on track.

In creating a plan to move forward, you will want to use the same SMART criteria you would use in creating a resolution to a conflict:

- Who will do what, when, and where? (**Specific**)
- How will you know a job is completed or a step has been accomplished? (**Measurable**)
- In the current environment, is the proposed action **possible**? (**Achievable**)
- Is it likely? (**Realistic**)
- How long is this plan or project going to take? (**Timed**)

By making The Exchange a normal part of your problem solving and decision making—and a standard element in your workplace's operation—you will change your organization for the better. You will create a culture of empowerment, shared responsibility, mutual understanding and accountability, higher morale, reduced turnover, and less stress. You'll also have fewer fires to put out—and you'll sleep better at night. What more could a manager want?

10

Using The Exchange with the People and Organizations You Serve

Patients don't file lawsuits because they've been harmed by shoddy medical care. Patients file lawsuits because they've been harmed by shoddy medical care and something else happens to them. That something else is "how they were treated, on a personal level, by their doctor."

—Malcolm Gladwell

The success of hospitals, restaurants, government agencies, nonprofit organizations, law offices, corporations with outside vendors, and of many other organizations depends not on the manufacturing of a widget but on the willingness of clients or customers to use their services again.

As a manager, you may be called on to clean up a conflict between one of your employees and someone who does not work for you, but who is nevertheless important to the running of your organization. When such conflicts flare up, the damage can be significant. You might wind up with a smaller pool of volunteers, a complaint to the Better Business Bureau, or a lawsuit.

As journalist Malcolm Gladwell points out, the actions that people take as the result of a less than satisfactory experience depend less on what happened than on how they were treated. This will serve as your guiding principle as you use The Exchange to resolve such conflicts.

The Exchange is not appropriate for every such conflict, of course, just as it isn't appropriate for every internal dispute. Large or serious conflicts (e.g., your employee and a customer get into a fistfight, or the driver of a supplier's delivery truck deliberately rear-ends an employee's car) will usually require formal mediation, arbitration, legal proceedings, or even intervention by the police. Legal liability may be a significant issue here, and it may be best to consult with your organization's lawyer before taking any action. Genuinely small conflicts can often best be resolved with a brief letter or phone call of apology (even if one is not really deserved), plus some simple gesture to make amends (e.g., a free gift certificate, the customer's next appointment at no charge, etc.). It's the in-between disputes—in which you're not worried about legal liability, but about good relationships with outside people and organizations—where The Exchange can be most helpful.

Part of what makes these situations difficult, however, is that you will have to deal with people over whom you have no authority. Nevertheless, you will use many of the same techniques of The Exchange, in many of the same ways.

These conflicts will require two meetings: a very brief private meeting with your employee, in which you will hear about the situation from their perspective, followed by a longer meeting with the outsider.

The first meeting will be a standard Stage I meeting, as described in Chapter 4.

In your meeting with the outsider, you will have the same general objectives as when you are dealing with an internal conflict: (1) establish rapport, (2) hear the person's perspective, (3) identify their interests, and (4) discuss what happens next. In most situations, this second meeting will be a hybrid of Stage I (learning the real source of the conflict) and Stage IV (problem solving), although in some cases you may be the only one supplying solutions.

Your employee will not be present at this second meeting. Instead, you will be their surrogate—or, at least, the person where the proverbial buck stops.

The easiest, most disarming, and most useful technique for quickly establishing rapport with the outsider is to simply introduce yourself and announce your intentions. Some examples:

- *Thanks for coming to this meeting. I'm the manager here, and I know things haven't gone the way you wanted or expected. I'm sorry that happened, and part of my job is to make sure that you feel the situation is adequately resolved—and that something similar doesn't happen again.*
- *Welcome. I'm _____, the department manager. My goal today is to listen, to understand, and to help repair the relationship between you and our organization.*

- *Good morning. I'm the manager here, and one big purpose of this meeting is to make things right. I appreciate your coming in, and I'm going to do everything I reasonably can to help you walk out of here satisfied.*

You won't need an icebreaker. In fact, in these situations, your stated willingness to make things right is almost always the best icebreaker. So, go straight to asking the outsider to explain the situation from their perspective. Then listen carefully and attentively.

As always, don't be too quick to offer a solution. Hear them out first, and let them express their emotions. Then let them know that you've heard them by quickly recapping what they said about what happened, as well as about how it affected them. This gives them a chance to cool down and move into a calmer, less reactive mood.

By now, the outsider may have made it very clear what kind of resolution they want. If you can safely and easily provide that resolution—for example, a straightforward apology and a promise to talk to your employee about their conduct—then by all means provide it. But always hear them out first.

Never assume you know what an outsider wants. In one situation we know about, an elderly resident of a nursing home slipped, fell, and broke her wrist in part because of inadequate signage. Staff was slow to find her, help her up, and get her to a doctor. Soon after her wrist was taken care of, her son came by to visit. She explained the incident, and he was understandably upset. He called the nursing home director and left a message on her voice mail, asking him to call her. What he wanted was an explanation, a brief apology, and an assurance that something similar wouldn't happen again. When the director called back a few hours later, however, her first words were, "Hello, Mr. Skinner, This is Kate Kosinski returning your call. How much money do you want?" Now he was outraged, because no one seemed to care about his mother or him.

Similarly, don't offer a solution of your own before giving the person a chance to fully describe what happened and how they feel about it. This may bring the meeting to a quick end, but you may miss the outsider's real interests. As a result, the "solution" may feel superficial and inadequate to them.

The outsider also needs to feel that the meeting has gone more or less the way they hoped it would. When the dynamics differ considerably from what they expect, they can feel uneasy.

Imagine that you go to an auto dealer to buy a new car. You've done lots of research, so you know exactly what car you want and what you can reasonably expect to pay for it. You shake the salesman's hand, point to the car you want, and make an offer on it. You know the offer is too low, but it's an appropriate place to begin negotiations. The salesman nods and says, "Sounds good. I'll write it up and get you the keys." How would you feel? In this situation, many people would wonder if they had made a mistake. Did they offer too much? Are they getting a lemon?

In resolving conflicts, the situation is often similar. If a solution is reached too quickly, before someone has had the chance to explain their viewpoint and tell their story, they may feel they didn't get a good deal.

As always, once the outsider has told their story, recap the main points you have heard, and ask to make sure you have understood everything the outsider wants you to hear. As part of this, say what you believe the person's interest is. For example:

> *When we didn't call back, you felt like we didn't care about you as a customer. Is that right?*
> Or, *You wanted a real person, not a machine, to actually hear you. Have I got that right?*
> Or, *You felt that our employee didn't treat you respectfully. Is that correct?*

Now you and the outsider can move into problem solving. But *don't* ask them what solution they'd like. That's too open a question. The outsider may say something like, "I want that employee fired" or "I want a year of free service." First of all, this request may simply be unreasonable; the outsider may be taking a negotiating position rather than genuinely trying to create a resolution. Second, the outsider's request may be beyond the scope of your authority. You then have to say no, and the outsider may feel disappointed, frustrated, and doubly rejected.

Instead, offer a tentative solution in a speculative, open-ended (rather than a prescriptive) way. If the outsider likes it, great. If not, and they have a better idea, you can be sure they will present it. For example:

> *Here's a thought. What if we were to assign the same customer service person to you from now on, so that you always knew who to call and talk to? I can give you their direct phone number, and I'll instruct them to personally handle all your inquiries from now on.*

What if we were to set aside the area behind the warehouse as a parking lot for trucks only? We'd put up a couple of "Trucks Only" signs, one at each end, and set up a line of cones in between. That ought to keep cars out of the area, and it will guarantee spots for at least three trucks. Would that work for you?

This is just an idea, but maybe it will solve things for you. I can have our delivery person start on the west side of town and move east, so that you always get your deliveries early in the morning instead of late in the afternoon. That way, if there's a problem with your shipment, you can call us in the morning, and we can make a new delivery by mid-afternoon. Would that solve the issue for you?

Now let's look at a few specific fields as examples of how to apply The Exchange in flexible and creative ways. We won't attempt sophisticated analyses; we're just illustrating the benefits of the tools and strategies discussed in this book. All these examples involve a manager, attempting to resolve a conflict with an important outsider.

HEALTH CARE

Professionals in the health care industry are often regarded as the experts—the keepers and purveyors of magic cures. When something goes wrong, however, they can easily become scapegoats. Furthermore, patients often have expectations and make demands that seem unreasonable to overworked nurses, physicians, or schedulers. As a result, whole conferences are devoted to managing conflicts.

Deborah Jonas is the chief administrator of a community clinic in a major city. This clinic is part of a very large hospital complex. One evening, Deborah hears shouting in the waiting room and quickly checks it out. She sees the front desk clerk in tears. An irate man holding a small boy shouts to the crowd of waiting people about his dissatisfaction. Evidently, he has been told that he missed his scheduled appointment and needs to make another one.

Deborah introduces herself as the clinic manager and invites the man and his son to take seats in her office, which is a few steps down the hall. Before joining them, however, she has a one minute conversation with the scheduler. She learns that the man was an hour late for a pediatric appointment and that the pediatrician they had expected to see had already left.

Deborah takes a deep breath, enters her office, and offers the father and son some water. Then she asks the man what happened. She learns that his son developed a severe earache the night before. The father called and scheduled an emergency appointment. Because of a mix-up with his wife about the car, however, and his inability to get a taxi quickly during rush hour, the two had to take a bus to the clinic. The man is almost frantic about his son, who is moaning quietly and obviously feverish.

Deborah expresses her concern about the boy and assures the father that someone will be available to see his son.

She calls the scheduler, finds out who is on duty and who is available, and books the next available slot. Smiling, she tells the father that Dr. Ibrahim, a family practitioner, will see the boy in 10 minutes. She suggests that they wait in her office.

Later, Deborah speaks to the front-desk staffer. She learns that there had been a series of belligerent patients demanding quick service that day; that two nurses had called in sick; and that the staffer felt utterly overwhelmed.

At the staff meeting the next day, Deborah raises three issues: scheduling, understaffing, and handling workplace stress. Privately, after the meeting, she assures the front-desk staffer that she is not going to be fired.

GOVERNMENT AGENCIES

Employees who staff the front desks at government agencies are particularly vulnerable to complaints from citizens, who sometimes blame the employees for anything the government does less than perfectly. The Exchange can provide these front-line folks with tools and skills that can reduce complaints and craft creative solutions.

In a large southwestern city, the Development Services Department is where builders and contractors go to get information about zoning and building codes, to submit plans for new construction projects, to get permission to begin work on those projects, to renew their licenses to work with the city, and to obtain all kinds of other permits and information.

Marcus, the deputy director of the department, oversees the permitting division. On a particularly busy afternoon, he hears one of the front-desk employees slam down the phone and declare, *Nobody talks to me like that.*

Marcus hurries out and asks the employee to come into his office, which is out of earshot of the people in the crowded lobby. He calmly asks the clerk to tell him just what happened. The clerk shakes his head and explains that an irate contractor who had many projects with the city had just cursed repeatedly at him. *All I did,* the clerk says, *is tell him the truth—that he needed another permit before beginning his work on the new convention center.* This is a huge, publicly funded construction project. *The guy threatened to call the City Council,* the clerk says. *He also threatened to have me fired. Then he called me a butthole and a dickless pencil-pusher.*

Marcus nods, promises that he will deal with the contractor, and sends his employee back to his station.

Marcus does not want to give the contractor enough time to carry out any of his threats. He quickly dials the contractor's number, ready to begin a modified Exchange. The contractor picks up the phone on the second ring. There is irritation in his voice even as he says hello.

Marcus introduces himself and quickly apologizes for the phone hang-up. *I've spoken to the employee,* he says. *The man was out of line. We should never hang up on anyone who does business with us. I'm sorry.* Then he says, *This is an important project for the city. I know you've worked with us to try to get your part of it started for months, tell me about the latest snag.*

In fact, Marcus knows exactly what that snag is. Newly passed state legislation requires another round of permitting; Marcus doesn't agree with the law, but of course knows he must uphold it. He keeps quiet while the contractor vents his frustration about being put on hold, dealing with incompetent staff, having to put off hiring workers, and so on and on.

When the contractor is done talking, Marcus says, *That's got to be incredibly frustrating—especially when it's all out of your hands and you can't do much to change things. I wish I had the power to wave a wand and make it better.* The contractor responds with a bitter laugh and says, *Yeah. It looks like we're both victims of the system.*

Marcus leverages this moment of commiseration. *Yeah,* he says, *we can't change the system, but sometimes we can create some shortcuts. Let's see what I can do to make your life easier.* The contractor perks up at that phrase and, within 5 minutes they develop a plan to combine a handful of procedures, which would normally take three visits to the department, into a single trip. The contractor isn't exactly happy, but he's grateful. *Thanks, man,* he says at the end of the conversation. *I wish more people in government were like you. Don't even get me started about the jerkwads down at the county. And one last thing: tell your phone guy I'm sorry I dissed him. I got nothing against him. He was just in the wrong place at the wrong time.*

SERVICE COMPANIES

Businesses that provide services—even the best-run ones—regularly get complaints from customers about how they are treated. The Exchange can be used effectively with most such complaints.

Although many restaurants go out of business after only a year or two, some develop a large and loyal customer base. One of those eateries is The Home Town Café, which specializes in comfort food.

Salim, the owner of The Home Town Café, used to let his staff take care of touchy situations with patrons. Now, however, if a customer even *looks* unhappy, Salim jumps into action, employing the techniques of The Exchange. First, he makes an effort to establish rapport by introducing himself and asking the customer their name. Then he asks about the situation and identifies his own interests: *It's very important to me that we have satisfied customers. So, please, tell me what happened.*

If the customer has a complaint, Salim makes no attempt to justify or explain anything. Instead, even when he thinks the customer is wrong, he demonstrates his understanding by paraphrasing the complaint. Then he acknowledges the impact of the situation on the customer. For example:

> *You came tonight to celebrate an important day for you. When the server moved you away from the table with the best view after you had already been seated, and then told you that the table was already reserved, you were very disappointed. I am so sorry this happened. I never want to disappoint anyone here.*

Salim then identifies the customer's interests, which almost always involve getting a tangible form of compensation—for example, a free dessert, a $10 gift certificate, or, for larger problems, their meal on the house. Salim knows that unhappy diners quickly become happy again—and often become repeat customers—when he uses these techniques from The Exchange.

NONPROFIT ORGANIZATIONS

In nonprofits, the contributions of volunteers are critical. Keeping loyal volunteers thus means treating them well and quickly addressing their concerns whenever a problem arises.

United Freedom Makers is a coalition of nonprofits that work with former convicts. The organization provides a smorgasbord of services, from gang-tattoo removal to therapy to job placement to counseling for families. All of UFM's participating agencies rely heavily on volunteers. UFM's board of directors includes many well-known lawyers, doctors, and other big community donors, as well as the directors of each of the coalition's member organizations.

Pat is the current head of the UFM Board of Directors, as well as the director of its family foundation group. One morning, immediately after a board meeting, Pat is accosted by Stan, an accomplished tattoo artist and the leader of the tattoo removal nonprofit. Stan threatens to resign because he was laughed at during the board meeting. At first Pat does not recall anyone laughing at Stan. Then, she remembers something a board member said—something Pat took as good-natured teasing. However, she knows that Stan is very sensitive; he has told her several times that he thinks other board members look down on him because he didn't finish high school.

Pat needs Stan on UFM's board. He's smart and a creative thinker, and he has a deep understanding of many of the issues ex-cons face, since he spent 2 years in jail himself many years ago, when he was in his early twenties. Also, the tattoo artists are great at PR and have added a lot of creative energy to fundraising efforts. So she says to him, *Stan, I could see that you were offended by that remark by Joan tonight. Is that why you want to resign?*

Stan says, *Hell, yes!* and then vents for a while about Joan, the rich, and the sense of entitlement among people with power and privilege. Pat listens, nodding. When Stan is done, she says, *You must know how important you are to this coalition. I've seen you go out of your way to help these teenage gangbangers find constructive activities and stay in school. What's going to happen to them if you quit?*

Reminded of his real interest (keeping teenagers out of jail), Stan calms down. He even acknowledges that "the suits" also care about keeping kids safe and out of trouble. The conversation ends with Stan agreeing to serve on UFM's special events committee, so that his tattoo-removal agency can host a community fundraising event.

As you become more practiced at using the strategies and techniques of The Exchange, they will eventually become part of the way you manage many situations. You'll get better and better at handling and preventing conflicts, and your work life will be that much richer for it.

11

About The Exchange and Its Creators

All humans are caught in an inescapable network of humanity, tied in a single garment of destiny. Whatever affects one directly, affects all indirectly.

—Martin Luther King, Jr., "Letter from a Birmingham Jail"

The Exchange did not spring from nothing. We recognize the importance of the people, organizations, and methods upon whose shoulders we stand.

The Exchange reflects the idea of personal connectedness that Dr. King recognized in the quotation above. Employees in a workplace have allies and connections, both within and beyond their worksite. A conflict at work can affect the families and communities in which the disputants live. The Exchange can also affect individuals, families, and communities—but in positive ways.

Although The Exchange is unique in its structure, it reflects important principles from many sources, especially principled negotiation and mediation. Principled negotiation stresses that, in order to be successful, negotiators need to recognize each other's interests—and to realize that their interests are interconnected. Mediation is built on empowerment, respect, and an awareness that its results affect far more people than the particular individuals who are directly involved.

FREQUENTLY ASKED QUESTIONS ABOUT THE EXCHANGE

When managers, administrators, HR professionals, and executives first learn about The Exchange, they often have a few questions. Here are the most common ones, and their answers.

1. **What was the original idea behind The Exchange?** The Exchange was created by NCRC trainers in order to provide the same structured approach to workplace conflicts that mediators use to resolve conflicts that have escalated into lawsuits. As mediation professionals, we have seen the enormous costs—financial, emotional, and otherwise—that result when leaders attempt to resolve conflicts using inadequate skills or ineffective strategies. We also recognize that most managers and supervisors do not have the time or money to invest in becoming professional mediators. Fortunately, they don't need to. In The Exchange, we have adapted a key piece of the formal mediation structure, the one that empowers clients to assess their own needs and make their own decisions. The Exchange makes this process informal and accessible to anyone who wants to resolve a dispute. Managers who consciously practice the techniques described in this book can reduce or eliminate many of the ongoing conflicts that infect most workplaces, both by resolving conflicts and by preventing them.

2. **What if I try The Exchange and it doesn't work?** The Exchange is not a magic bullet—nor is it a stand-alone process. It has been used to resolve innumerable conflicts, but it will not succeed every time, and it is not the only approach to conflict worth employing. In fact, we at NCRC view The Exchange as one key piece of an organization's Integrated Conflict Management System (ICMS). We have designed ICM systems for many large organizations. Generally, these involve multiple processes that address internal conflicts at three or four different levels. In Level I, a worried or affronted person speaks directly and informally to another in an attempt to resolve the situation one to one. At Level II, a manager, administrator, or HR professional facilitates The Exchange. At Level III, disputants participate in a formal mediation process conducted by a trained neutral (usually from outside the organization). In Level IV, the dispute is submitted to

arbitration. Most workplace disputes can be resolved at Level II by using The Exchange.

3. **What about those disruptive, conflict-prone people in a workplace who are always fighting with someone, yet who have important skills—or who have tenure or some other vested place in the organization? How do we deal with such people, who are impossible to work with and impossible to fire?** These people typically have traits of what mediator Bill Eddy calls high conflict personalities. (Bill has written an excellent book on the subject called *It's All Your Fault: 12 Tips for Managing People Who Blame Others for Everything.*) In general, people with these traits are not swayed by debate, argument, logic, or attempts to appeal to their sense of fairness. Very often these folks simply do not have the capacity for self-reflection. They aren't trying to be difficult; they are simply convinced that their point of view is the only right or valid one. We've learned that, with these folks, The Exchange sometimes settles the conflict, sometimes not. It most cases, however, using the communication skills embedded in The Exchange (listen effectively, respond respectfully, and go deeper with open questions) does de-escalate the situation considerably. This often allows the manager to move the conversation away from denial and blame, and toward some form of resolution. (Typically, this involves employing preexisting criteria such as organizational policy, legal requirements, or organizational precedent for dealing with such situations.) see pp. 94–97, Adapting the Exchange for Disruptive People.

4. **What if people just don't want to meet together? Maybe they're too scared, or embarrassed, or they just don't want to be in the same room together.** In some cases, if you have the authority, it may make sense to overrule the employees and insist on a joint meeting. In others, you may choose to modify the joint meeting by becoming a "shuttle diplomat," with each disputant in a different room. This takes more time than a standard joint meeting, but we've seen it work quite well. (In such situations, eventually the two people usually do sit down together.) The danger of shuttle diplomacy is that you may inadvertently become enmeshed in the conflict if someone doesn't like the messages they receive. Another danger is someone accusing you of misinterpreting or misrepresenting their message. One way to avoid such a trap is to repeat aloud the message you plan to take before you deliver it, and ask whether you're presenting it

accurately. Once a message is approved, you can then deliver it word for word.

5. **What if I have a problem with my boss? I can handle my employees, but I just don't know how to approach her.** In such situations, of course, you cannot be a neutral, third-party facilitator. If someone in your organization with the appropriate authority has used The Exchange, you can ask them to facilitate the process between you and your boss. If this isn't possible, you can try to find someone above your boss on the organizational chart who is willing to read this book and use The Exchange for the first time. If this isn't feasible, you can ask your boss for a one-to-one meeting to discuss the situation that is bothering you. This meeting won't (and can't) closely resemble either a one-to-one meeting or a group session as used in The Exchange. However, in it you can still use some of the speaking, listening and planning techniques that help make The Exchange work. For example:

   - Ask to meet at a time when your boss will be relatively relaxed and not facing distractions or other people's immediate demands.
   - Ask to meet in a private location where no one can observe your interaction, so that your boss cannot lose face in front of other employees.
   - When you meet, begin by very briefly describing the situation that concerns you. Then, rather than describing the situation in detail, speak openly about how it is affecting you—especially your ability to be productive.
   - As much as possible, describe the issues in ways that don't escalate it or place blame on your boss.
   - Don't confront your boss about their inadequacies. Instead, ask them what they would like to see from you in order to improve the situation. This is a subtle way of both sharing your interests and asking them to share theirs.

   If your boss has a disruptive or high-conflict personality, these techniques may or may not work. Take heart, however. We know of two employees of bullying bosses who were eventually promoted to take their bosses' places—after those bosses were fired. Both people used the skills they learned in The Exchange to de-escalate many conflicts.

6. **What if I want more training in this field?** NCRC offers several training options in mediation and conflict resolution, from the

introductory to the advanced level. **For details about the Exchange, visit www.exchangetraining.com.** We also offer a formal certification program in mediation. For details, visit www.ncrconline.com.

ABOUT THE NATIONAL CONFLICT RESOLUTION CENTER

Under several names, NCRC has provided mediation, facilitation, and conflict resolution training since 1983. Headquartered in San Diego, California, NCRC is one of the largest full-service conflict resolution centers in the United States—and it is the first to have developed a mediator credential based on training, experience and performance. NCRC provides both pro bono community mediation and fee-based conflict resolution through several professional panels of specialist mediators. Its newest division, the West Coast Resolution Group, provides mediation and dispute resolution services to the legal community. **For details, visit www. westcoastresolution.com.**

NCRC's trainers have developed and taught seminars in North and South America, Europe, and Asia. NCRC also offers trainings in The Exchange for executives, managers, students, and community members. These trainings can be adapted for organizations of all types.

NCRC has trained thousands of people to resolve disputes in legal, corporate, community, and family settings. Its motto is "There *is* a solution."

NCRC's professionals are not academics or theorists. They are problem solvers who have worked with real people in real conflicts.

To learn more about NCRC, or to attend one of its upcoming trainings, visit its Web site, **www.ncrconline.com.**

Index